GOSPELED
Lives

GOSPELED Lives

Encounters with Jesus

A LENTEN STUDY

JOHN INDERMARK

UPPER
ROOM BOOKS®
NASHVILLE

GOSPELED LIVES: Encounters with Jesus
Copyright © 2008 by John Indermark
All rights reserved.

Cover design: Bruce Gore / Gore Studio / www.gorestudio.com
Cover image: Steven D. Purcell
Typesetting: PerfecType, Nashville, TN

LIBRARY OF CONGRESS CATALOGING-IN-PUBLICATION DATA
Indermark, John
    Gospeled lives : encounters with Jesus : a Lenten study / John Indermark.
        p. cm.
    ISBN 978-0-8358-9971-0 (print) | ISBN 978-0-8358-1658-8 (mobi) | ISBN 978-0-8358-1659-5 (epub)
    1. Jesus Christ—Biography—History and criticism. 2. Bible. N.T. Gospels—Criticism, interpretation, etc. I. Title.
    BT301.3. I53 2008
    242'.34—dc22   2008025026

To the

Writers and Editors
of
Seasons of the Spirit

Colleagues, Friends, Community

CONTENTS

ACKNOWLEDGMENTS

Books do not come out of nowhere—or perhaps, if they do, that may be where they are headed. And while I hope you do not decide "nowhere" is the destination of this work, I can say without fear of contradiction that it has its sources in many places and persons.

The one responsible for taking this from offered proposal to accepted project is my former acquisitions editor at Upper Room Books, JoAnn Miller. Without her advocacy on this as on earlier book projects, these words might not have seen the light of day. From JoAnn's hands they passed into the care of Robin Pippin, the current acquisitions editor, for further shepherding through the process. I am especially grateful for the editing work of Jeannie Crawford-Lee in moving from manuscript to completed book.

Paying my dues to those who have contributed to my understanding and experience of a "gospeled" life involves a host of characters from my recent and distant past. Parish teachers Lillian Schaefer and Faye Chall and Pastor Jesse Pollmann; lay leaders and workers in churches I have served such as Bonnie and Gene Adams, Roger and Carol King, Martha Mundt, Slim and Helen Crenshaw, Anna Ehrulund and Francy Penttila; colleagues in ministry like Phil Eisenhower, Lynn Longfield, Joel Biggers, Ruth Mathis, and Donald Schmidt; my parents and grandparents: all these and many others have provided examples of lives transformed and transforming through encounter with the Holy in life.

The witness of communities to gospeled lives has also shaped the direction of this book by shaping me. The dedication page has already called attention to the gatherings of writers and editors who come together to fashion the *Seasons in the Spirit* lectionary curriculum. Do not think it is merely a group charged with a task. Through weeklong encounters with the biblical texts in word and art and song; by speaking out of our perspectives; and by listening to the experiences of faith from quite diverse individuals and places and nations, we become, well, the church. Congregations I have grown up in, whether as a child, as a pastor, or now as an ordained member of the laity, have shed light—and sometimes a little shadow—on what it means for lives to be gospeled. I remain grateful for all the experiences gained there that form the background out of which I write. Over the years, what I write has been aided and abetted by participation in a group of writers who gather to read and critique one another's writings and generally enjoy one another's company: Jenelle Varila, Brian Harrison, and Bryan Penttila.

Finally, I am able to engage in the ministry of writing because of the support of my wife and partner and often first editor of the text, Judy Indermark.

To all these, this book is indebted for whatever wisdom you may find in it for your journey in faith—and what light it might shed on what it means for your own experience of a life gospeled by encounter with God.

USING THIS BOOK

Why This Title, This Book

The title *Gospeled Lives* may sound odd to modern ears. In English, *gospel* serves as a noun and occasionally an adjective. The Greek of the New Testament, though, often uses a verb form of the word we translate as *gospel*. *Gospel* can express action. "Gospeled" lives are lives profoundly affected by an encounter with Jesus. Gospeled lives do not always veer the same direction. The chapter titles reflect the diverse components of such encounter as well as the responses it may evoke. Calls may be heard or neglected. Challenges may be taken on or passed up. Transformation may be embraced or avoided. Some people leave the encounter unpersuaded. Others depart empowered. In every case, the story of gospeled lives remains open-ended. That is, response to encounter with Jesus continues to unfold in ongoing choices and unfinished stories. The book intentionally ends on that note, for that is where you and I enter the picture. Our lives write the yet-to-be lived stories of our response to encounter with Jesus.

This book offers an opportunity to revisit encounters with Jesus by the characters who people the stories in Matthew, Mark, and Luke. Omitted are stories in the Gospel of John covered in my earlier book *Companions in Christ: The Way of Grace,* along with some characters considered in *Neglected Voices.* I believe folks hunger for connections between the biblical word and their lives. Those of us in mainline traditions often give lip service to that desire but do not always follow through. The Gospels' stories of encounter with Jesus provide a healthy "buffet" for that hunger, allowing us the opportunity to overhear our own experiences in these stories.

Guidelines for Using This Book

Gospeled Lives is intended to be read over a six-week period in the season of Lent, one chapter per week. The prologue offers a story of encounter that sets the stage for those that follow. For each week, an overview presents the week's theme, followed by five daily readings. You may want to read the overview the first day of the week, the five readings on each of the next five days, and then observe a weekly sabbath from reading. Perhaps that last day might be spent reading the overview once more and reflecting on what you read. For those participating in a group study, use this sabbath for your group meeting day.

Each daily reading consists of a text reference to a character's encounter with Jesus, a reading that grows out of that narrative of encounter, a brief prayer, and a suggested exercise entitled "Encountering Jesus Today." Please read the scripture passage first. It sets the stage for the reading, prayer, and experience that follows. Do not neglect the daily "Encountering Jesus Today" exercises. Doing these exercises leads you to connect the reading with your own spiritual journey and growth. Be aware that these exercises intentionally blend reflection with action in response to the readings. Spiritual formation takes place when we both internalize and externalize the faith. In more traditional language, we are called to be hearers and doers of the word—and of the grace and call we encounter in Jesus.

If you will be leading or assisting a group study of this book (or are just curious!), session instructions follow in the Leader's Guide. If you are reading this book independently, you might use the session guides as one way to reflect on your thoughts and experiences growing out of each week's readings.

Prologue

It was carved in the front of the Communion Table at First Christian Church in Olympia where I preached yesterday. I have seen it stitched into cloths draped over altars and Communion Tables in other sanctuaries I have entered in hopes of holy encounter. "In Remembrance of Him." Whenever we gather at that table, we do so in remembrance of Christ. And that is good.

But here is what I have never seen carved into wooden pulpits or stitched on the fabric draping them: "In Remembrance of Her." And that is not good. Why? That neglect signifies we have forgotten the teaching of Jesus: "Truly I tell you, where this good news [gospel] is proclaimed in the whole world, what she has done will be told in remembrance of her."

Who is this "her" whose remembrance we have not always or even often kept wherever the gospel is preached? Why does her story of encounter with Jesus precede and illuminate our remembering the other characters in this book?

She is the woman who anoints Jesus. While all four Gospels differ over the details of her encounter, including her identity, they all agree upon the extravagance of this woman's action. She takes an expensive imported ointment and pours it out upon Jesus' head or feet, depending upon which account you read. The witnesses who say "feet" include a description of her wiping Jesus' feet with her hair. The intimate—and scandalous—nature of her action is without parallel in the Gospels. In her encounter with Jesus, devotion takes extravagant form.

Objections immediately arise. Luke alone notes the objection made to this physical contact with Jesus, even as Luke alone identifies her as "a woman of the city who was a sinner." The other Gospels focus the protests on her wastefulness and Jesus' allowing

13

her to indulge in such a lavish squandering of money. To which Jesus responds: "You always have the poor with you, *but you do not always have* me" (emphasis added).

In Jesus' eyes, this woman has not repudiated the poor. Those who think her action justifies indifference to the vulnerable among us forget that Jesus' parable of the great judgment stands only a few verses previous in Matthew 25:31-46. This woman has ministered to Jesus in a way best described as *gracious*. After all, a *wise* use of the ointment would have been to save or invest it. A *charitable* use would have been to sell it and give its proceeds to the poor. A *practical* use would have been to trade it for some needed item. Instead, this woman chooses a *gracious* use by her extravagant gesture. The loving and gracious God whom Jesus came to reveal finds witness in this woman's action toward Jesus. Jesus bids us remember her wherever the gospel is preached because her action *is* its preaching.

To be sure, the woman's encounter also brings grace to her from Jesus. But that grace takes shape in more than Jesus' defense of her before critics or his invocation to remember her. Prior to these declarations, Jesus graced her with the opportunity to express devotion. After all, what if, as the woman opens the perfume and unclasps her hair, Jesus stops her and says: *No, no, this isn't necessary. You don't have to do this. I know of your love.* Would the lesson then be: love needs no expression as long as it is understood?

Jesus graces this woman's life by indulging her with the opportunity to demonstrate love. He does not stop it short. Jesus does not minimize its cause or need. Jesus allows it to happen. Jesus proves as hospitable to grace in the receiving as in the giving. That may not be an easy example for us to follow. We are raised to embrace the grace of God to us. We are not always so good at the practice of accepting grace from another person. We want to be in control. We want to be in charge. We discover the downside to the blessedness of giving over receiving when we find it difficult to allow others to be giving toward us. Yet that is the grace Jesus bestows upon her: to act with love and grace to the one who came as grace and love incarnate.

"What she has done will be told in remembrance of her." Her story thus serves as a fitting entry into this book's explorations of other encounters with Jesus. We do so in remembrance of these individuals in order to see the "gospeling" of their lives through encounter with Jesus.

But make no mistake: the goal of telling stories "in remembrance of them"—both in the Gospels and in this book—is the hope for our own life-changing encounter with Christ. Such hope hinges on our hearing the gospel's call. Such hope relies on accepting the challenges the gospel inevitably brings. Such hope turns on our not turning a deaf ear or hard heart or closed mind to those in whom we may encounter the Christ. Such hope proves receptive to transformation as a welcomed if not always comfortable way of life rather than a feared change of the status quo. Such hope seeks God's empowerment to live anew. Such hope remain open to a God whose habit is surprise, whose desire is justice and peace, and whose fundamental disposition toward creation is love.

Such a God stands ready to encounter us in scriptured word and living Christ. May we now find in these remembrances the hope of life discovered through encounter with Jesus.

Open me, O God, to these storied remembrances and to gospeled encounter with You.

ENCOUNTERING JESUS TODAY

Reread the story of the woman who anoints Jesus. What do you find yourself remembering about her? Why? Think about yourself. If your life ended today, what would others "remember" most about you? Prayerfully reflect on what you would hope to be remembered for. Identify one or two actions you can take this week, and beyond, to fashion that remembrance.

Week One

CALLED

THE VOICES OF OUR MOTHERS would sound over the fences and into the yards where we played. Smells from deep fryers scalding French fries in oil accompanied that summons to mealtime. Failing light in the sky linked the callings to bedtime. Flashes of lightning punctuated verbal reminders to get in out of the rain. A firmer voice recalled you to homework or a family commitment. Hearing your name in any case meant it was time to go. And woe to those for whom the call had to be repeated—or included one's middle name!

But whether for the children in my St. Louis neighborhood or for the individuals who encountered Jesus in Galilee or Judea: to be called is to be singled out for the purpose of a response. In the case of Jesus, that call and its desired response need not always take the exact same form. The call may be an invitation to follow. The call may evoke an admission of the need for grace. The call may ask, *What do you want me to do for you?* The call may be to carry another's burden. The call may be to open oneself to a never-conceived possibility and then to risk trusting that possibility and telling others about it. Call, like faith, has everything to do with response. Gospel encounters with Jesus hinge on response to those calls.

Indeed, "call" provides the name for Christian community. "Church" translates the Greek word *ekklesia*, whose literal meaning is "called out." Faithful response to encounter with Christ creates the community of the called. Listen, then, in this season of Lent, to stories of lives gospeled by encounter with Jesus. In listening, may you attend to the voice sounding your own name and calling you to faithful response today.

DAY ONE

Simon and His Partners   *Luke 5:1-11*

Do you remember the television show *Columbo*? The lead character, Detective Columbo, has a curious habit. His questioning of suspects or witnesses proceeds innocently enough. Straightforward. He thanks them for their time, starts to head out the door, and then suddenly stops and turns; he says there's just one more little thing he needs to know. And usually this last-minute flash in his mind is truly the most important question of all. He takes people into his confidence, or lets them think he is a bumbler, and then springs what he is *really* after when they let down their guard.

I had never thought of Columbo as a Christ figure until I started playing with this text from Luke in preparation for writing. This story of the fishermen's call differs greatly from the accounts in Matthew and Mark on one significant point. The way both these Gospels tell it, Jesus is walking by the sea, sees the fishermen, and out of the blue says, "Follow me." Lo and behold, they do. Immediately. They do so without having witnessed any acts of Jesus' public ministry that might justify their instantaneous response. Jesus speaks. They follow.

That is a powerful call story. But it is not the one Luke tells.

Luke prefaces this story by indicating reports about Jesus are spreading around the country. Jesus had already stirred up a commotion in his home of Nazareth, so much so that the hometown crowd determined to take Jesus to the nearest cliff and give him a push. From there he went to Capernaum, a city on the Sea of Galilee's northwest shore. After attending synagogue and startling people with an act of healing (on the sabbath, no less), Jesus visited the home of a woman who was ill with fever. He cured her as well. We do not know her name, only that of her son-in-law: a fisherman named Simon, later called Peter. So when our text notes Jesus gets into Simon's boat, he does not do so as a stranger. And he does not do so, at least initially, to invite Simon to follow. He needs a boat to go out on the water where he can speak to the crowds.

That's all he asks of Simon—just the use of his boat. At first.

But when the sermon's over and it's time to head ashore, the "Columbo" Jesus shows up. *Oh, by the way, before we go in, why don't you head out to deeper water and put out your nets for a catch. Could you do that?* Several factors are at work here. For starters, you have a land-based carpenter (we have no legends about Jesus as a fisherman) telling a fishing captain what to do. Secondly, the novice suggests using the nets, and the Greek word translated as "nets" refers to the kind used only at night. It's daytime. Simon and his partners had just spent the night on the lake, with those same nets, unsuccessfully. You begin to wonder if Simon and his crew might suddenly have gained some sympathy with the folks of Nazareth who wanted to do away with this erstwhile rabbi. They wouldn't have to find a cliff. Over the side of the boat would do just fine. But in a way that hints at Simon's streak of curiosity, if not openness to trying out new paths, he agrees to Jesus' direction. Nets are cast. Fish are hauled. And have you noticed something? Jesus still hasn't gotten around to calling Simon and his partners to follow. In Luke, the call does not come out of the blue. The call comes out of healing a loved one, spending time, and issuing instructions that should have proved futile but instead have proved fruitful. Only then does Jesus get to the call at hand: "Do not be afraid; from now on you'll be catching people." Only then do Simon and his partners leave everything behind and follow Jesus.

The narratives of the fishermen's call in Matthew and Mark focus on the startling and miraculous way in which a man who is practically a stranger calls—and response comes immediately. The call story in Luke includes startling and miraculous details, to be sure. But at the core, the call comes from one already known.

A colleague in a neighboring town pursues dual vocations of Episcopal priest and commercial fisher. Besides that, Irene is a writer to boot. One of her books is *Sea Fire: Tales of Jesus and Fishing.* Her comments there on fishing communities, born from academic research and years of living and working in the fishing industry, illustrate the core of Luke's call story:

> Fishing communities tend to be subcultures within a dominant culture. They are suspicious of outsiders. Only by taking part in their daily routines could Jesus have gained the trust and confidence of those fishermen whom he then recruited as his disciples.

Jesus worshiped among the fishermen. Jesus healed one of their own. Jesus spent time on the water with them. Only after laying that groundwork (or, seawork) did Jesus issue a call.

Jesus still calls us to follow by first preparing the way. We do not find ourselves addressed by a stranger, one whom we have never heard or seen before. The possibility of trust and our answering yes to Jesus is enhanced by knowing the One who speaks our name and invites us to follow.

This is a lesson we would do well to heed as individuals and communities of faith. If we follow that call to be fishers of people, we need not come at folks out of the blue with our words or invitations. We, too, need to do the groundwork. We too need to be part of another's life if we are to know how and where Christ's grace might best be offered and needed. People do not follow strangers. People follow those they trust, and who share life with them.

That is how Christ has called us—and calls us still.

Help me to hear your call, O God, not only from on high—but from close by. Amen.

Encountering Jesus Today

Imagine Jesus has said he would join you for an hour this day. Where would you most like Christ to be with you? What would you like to be able to do? How might Christ's presence change something you do today? Go ahead and make that change. Christ is with you.

Day Two

Death and taxes, so say some, are the only inevitabilities in life. So perhaps it was inevitable that a tax collector would be among those called by Jesus. Inevitability, however, does not guarantee respectability. Tax collectors in Jesus' day were little more than financial bounty hunters who paid Rome the equivalent of franchise fees to collect taxes in a given district. Any excess collected beyond the cost of the fee and Rome's assessment was pure profit. Since personal prosperity directly linked to the amount extracted, tax collectors earned a well-deserved reputation for ruthlessness. They also gained a disgraced standing in the eyes of Jewish society.

Tax collectors could not give testimony in court. Neither they nor their families could hold office in the community. Some rabbis held that just as you could lie to a robber to avoid theft, so you were justified in lying to a tax collector to avoid loss. In terms of the "classes" of that day's society, tax collectors were routinely lumped together in the same category with thieves. Finally, this dishonor for Gentile tax collectors only multiplied for any Jew who betrayed his own people by becoming a Roman hireling.

"After this [Jesus] went out and saw a tax collector named Levi, sitting at the tax booth." In the verse right before this story, Luke had recorded the crowd's amazement at a healing by Jesus with these words: "we have seen strange things today" (Luke 5:26).

The day is about to get a lot stranger. Jesus says to this tax collector: "Follow me." Levi (also known as Matthew) "left everything and followed him." No explanation for why Jesus calls this scoundrel. No rationale for why Levi responds so abruptly and completely. It just happens. And it gets stranger. Levi invites Jesus to a banquet at his house—"and there was a large company of tax collectors and others with them."

Eating in public then was not the casual exercise it is today. We give no thought to who may be seated at the table next to us at Sizzler's or Burger King. If we admit to any philosophical spin about our dining habits, we might throw about the adage, "you are what you eat." In Jesus' time, however, the more pertinent axiom would be, *you are those with whom you eat.* Family ties were expressed and deepened by family meals. Friendship bonds were revealed by your table companions. Meals shared with lowlifes and ne'er-do-wells reflected on your character.

So we may sympathize with righteous-minded Pharisees who take offense at this situation. "Why do you eat and drink with tax collectors and sinners?" Sometimes the Pharisees get a bad rap for legalistic nit-picking in the Gospels. This is not the case here. Theirs is the natural question to ask. *Don't you know what sort of people these are? Don't you care about community standards?* They ask the question, I dare say, that would run through many minds today were it our teacher, our minister, our standard-bearer, who sat at table with folks more familiar to the sheriff's department than the sewing circle. Why does Jesus eat with *those* people?

"Those who are well have no need of a physician, but those who are sick; I have come to call not the righteous but sinners to repentance." I confess some uncertainty about how satisfying Jesus' answer was then—and is now. It might be hard to justify his recklessness with a missional perspective; that is, Jesus ate with these people because he came to help the sick and the sinful. Like the chaplain of a downtown rescue mission working with addicts and derelicts, Jesus ministered to the down-and-out. The problem with that explanation is that in worldly standards his tax-collector dinner companions were hardly the down-and-out. Preaching *at* them might seem the more respectable thing to do than eating *with* them. But is the point here respectability, or is it call? I myself am not convinced Jesus' words alleviated the concerns of respectable and righteous Pharisees—or their kin among us today. I am not sure his words were even intended to do so. Jesus' response to them—and to us—entails admitting our need for grace.

Grace was the basis for Jesus' call of Levi. Unless Jesus needed someone gifted at handling the books or extracting contributions from the crowds, there seems no other explanation. Grace was the basis for Jesus' breaking bread with the disreputable of his time, the very sort of ones we point out to our children and say: *that's what could happen to you if you make bad choices or hang around in the wrong company.* Ironically such grace that calls Levi and practices table fellowship with those other characters is the same grace that aims to include the offended righteous. Self-avowed states of righteousness can close us off from recognizing the need for grace in our lives. Jesus was not disinterested in good and righteous folk. Rather, his overarching concern was—and is—to reach those in need of grace.

Call finds response from those who recognize their need for gracious acceptance. Righteousness is not a yardstick to separate us from others. Righteousness comes as a gift from Christ, who reconciles us not only with God but with all the other characters Christ joins at table and calls to follow.

Inviting God, free me to receive your call and respond to your grace that seeks us all. In Jesus Christ. Amen.

Encountering Jesus Today

Put yourself in Levi's shoes and read Luke 5:27-32. What is your experience of Jesus? Put yourself in the shoes of the Pharisees and read Luke 5:27-32. What is your experience of Jesus? Read Luke 5:27-32 as if it was intended for you alone. What is your experience of Jesus?

Day Three

Bartimaeus   *Mark 10:46-52*

In Mark, a blind beggar named Bartimaeus calls on Jesus to have mercy on him. In Luke, an unnamed beggar calls on Jesus to have mercy on him. In Matthew, two unnamed beggars call on Jesus to have mercy on them. Do the Gospels narrate two or even three separate incidents? Or is this one event variously remembered? Such questions of detail remain unanswered. But two details and one question are constants in every account. They all begin with the blind one(s) sitting by the "way" (the literal meaning of the word translated in the New Revised Standard Version as "roadside"). They all end with the blind one(s) following Jesus—Mark adds that he "followed Jesus on the *way* (same word)." How the blind one(s) got from sitting *by* the way to following *on* the way centers in Jesus' question common to all accounts: "What do you want me to do for you?"

There is no small irony in Jesus' asking this question. Not many verses before (Mark 10:36), Jesus had asked this same question almost verbatim of James and John. They had come requesting the equivalent of a blank check ("Teacher, we want you to do for us whatever we ask of you"). Jesus' question sought to clarify what they really were asking for. Here, Bartimaeus begins by asking for mercy. But what does he mean by mercy? After all, the word for "mercy" and the word for "alms"—an older term for charitable contributions—share the same root. Was this beggar asking for mercy as in a few coins dropped his way? Or did "mercy" stand for something else? Jesus asks the question. Mark has suggested earlier that Jesus understands what is in the minds of others (2:8). So is the question for Jesus' sake, so that he can know for sure what the individual wants? Or is there another purpose: for Bartimaeus to be able to identify what he truly seeks in his request for mercy?

At this point, imagine Jesus is asking you instead of Bartimaeus: "What do you want me to do for you?" Think about your life at this time. What would your answer be? What would you want Jesus to do for you? If this feels uncomfortable or awkward, consider that you answer this question every time you offer prayer to God in the name of Christ. In intercession for yourself and others and the world around you, you are naming what you want Jesus to do. You are naming what you mean by mercy.

But how is Jesus' question to Bartimaeus connected to this chapter's theme of call? In his book *Wishful Thinking*, Frederick Buechner speaks of vocation (calling) as "the place where your deep gladness and the world's deep hunger meet." Let me also suggest that empathy for and even awareness of those deep needs of the world require a prior recognition of our own deep needs. Otherwise, our calling becomes a doing "for" others what we somehow deny about ourselves. Jesus' question "What do you want me to do for you?" provides an opportunity for this individual—and for us—to name such need. To the credit of Bartimaeus, he does not request a potful of money so that he can go home for a day or week or even the rest of his life and not worry again. Bartimaeus speaks his fundamental need this way: "let me see again."

"What do you want me to do for you?" Again, what would you answer for yourself? What need do you have, the empty spot in the depth of your being, that stands in the way of the deep gladness Buechner speaks of—or in the way of empathy for others? What would let you, like Bartimaeus, "see" again or see for the first time?

As elsewhere in the Gospel of Mark, there is no extended dialogue or reflection. Jesus simply declares Bartimaeus's faith has made him well or saved him; the Greek verb means both. Two realities immediately change for Bartimaeus. First, he regains his sight. Second, he follows Jesus. No longer sitting *by* the way, no longer being *in* the way as the disciples' initial "shushing" implied, Bartimaeus is now *on* the way. It is worth mentioning that one of the earliest metaphors for the community who followed Jesus was "the Way." Bartimaeus is now on that way. Perhaps Mark names him because Bartimaeus was a specific individual known in the community addressed by this Gospel.

The experience of call for Bartimaeus begins in Jesus' question that invites recognition and confession of need. Notice I did not say recognition and confession of sin. Sometimes we in the church put such a premium on our need for God's forgiveness that we manage to avoid other needs we bear. Many of us are well-versed in offering a confession of sin. But Jesus' question is not aimed at the sins of Bartimaeus or our own. "What do you want me to do for you?" beckons in a different direction. The question calls us to identify what would make us whole by naming the need that separates us from God and from others. In that call, it prepares us to follow like Bartimaeus in response to a grace that saves and makes us whole.

So called and so restored, the one who started out sitting by the way became one who followed on the way. So called and so restored, that can be our story and our way as well.

"What do you want me to do for you?"

Jesus, remove from my way whatever keeps me from your way.

Encountering Jesus Today

Write a prayer in which you confess your need of God. But in this prayer, do not confess your sin. Let the confession address other places in your life. Do this not because you are without sin but because not all your needs arise from sin. Write your words with Jesus' question in mind: "What do you want me to do for you?" Write your words with Bartimaeus' example in mind. Pray this prayer each morning for the next week.

DAY FOUR

Highway 101 on the Oregon coast south of Yachats possesses a striking combination of incredible scenery and blind curves. The former beckoned my wife and me to vacation there one winter week. The latter compelled us to take actions and follow courses we had not planned on.

As we drove uphill toward a curve arcing alongside a steep ocean-side cliff, another vehicle came around that curve on the ocean side, then drifted into our lane. I braked hard, veering into a narrow shoulder lined by a guard rail and braced for impact. It never happened. Instead, the other car hit the rail ahead of us and went airborne, landing on the side bank beside and below us. Judy and I scrambled down and found the driver unconscious. Another car stopped, and we shouted at them to find a phone and call an ambulance (pre-cellular days). Unsure whether the victim had sustained spinal injuries, we knew enough not to try twisting him out. But did we know enough to help? He stopped breathing several times. Judy would lean in the window and yell at him to take a breath, and he would. This went on for what seemed like an hour, though I believe the ambulance arrived within twenty minutes followed by the State Patrol. We gave statements to the officer and the medical crew, then looked on in disbelief when the medics declared the man deceased. Probably a heart attack, they said, figuring that's what caused him to cross lanes. With nothing more needed from us, the officials sent us on our way. It was a changed way. Not long after that, Judy became an Emergency Medical Technician. Some time later, I became an ambulance driver and drove for ten years. It all traced back, in my understanding, to that chance encounter.

Scripture does not tell us why this man named Simon was out on Jerusalem's streets that day. Mark keeps the details about Simon to a bare minimum: a passerby coming in from the country, from the city of Cyrene (North Africa); the father of Alexander and Rufus. We get the impression that this individual just happened to be in the wrong place at the wrong time. Simon does not carry the cross of Jesus out of choice but out of compulsion. It was a one-time duty—and when it was done, the guards likely sent Simon on his way. But was it a changed way?

That is the question behind the inclusion of Simon of Cyrene in a chapter about "call." Clearly Jesus did not call out to this individual and request a helping hand. It is highly improbable the Romans asked Simon whether he cared to do this or not. More likely, they pressed Simon into service so a fresh back could get them to Golgotha more quickly, and they'd be done with the assignment ASAP. Where is call in that?

To me, the connection of Simon and call begins in the reminder that not all calls we receive in life or faith are freely chosen, at least in their origins. While I suppose my wife and I could have driven on after witnessing that car accident, I don't recall either of us giving that any thought. We felt compelled to stay, even after law enforcement and medical aid arrived. It was like we needed to find out about this man, and what would happen. When told he was dead, it was even harder to leave then, a bit like the way mourners linger at a graveside after the services have concluded.

So I wonder about Simon of Cyrene. Having borne that cross up the rise called Golgotha, did he drop it there and leave? Did he stay? Did he seek out some word about who this was whose cross he had just carried, and, perhaps, whose death he witnessed?

We do not know for sure. But two details suggest such a connection, and even an association with call. The first is Mark's observation that Simon was the father of Alexander and Rufus. Mark is not in the habit of naming folks whose lives only briefly intersect with Jesus. Like his naming of Bartimaeus in the previous reading, mentioning these names may suggest the individuals were known to the community Mark addressed. A tantalizing clue appears in Paul's letter to the church at Rome, a community often associated with the composition of Mark's Gospel. In that letter Paul sends greetings to "Rufus, chosen in the Lord" (Rom. 16:13).

But an even more provocative clue associating this story with call comes in Mark's choice of the word "passer-by." Mark uses this Greek word in only two other places in this Gospel. The first is 1:16: "As Jesus *passed along* the Sea of Galilee, he saw Simon." The second is 2:14: "As [Jesus] was *walking along*, he saw Levi." In both cases, the word becomes a precursor to call. For Simon by the sea and Levi at the tax booth, the call came from Jesus. For Simon of Cyrene, the call came under compulsion from soldiers. But in all these instances those calls resulted in bearing the cross of Jesus, figuratively or literally.

Simon of Cyrene was compelled to carry Jesus' cross on that one day. Circumstances in our lives sometimes force us to take actions we would not have chosen and might prefer never having to face again. The question is: do we merely put up with such duress for the moment and then go on with our lives as if it never happened? Or do we open ourselves to ways in which those experiences—and our responses—change our course and perhaps those who come after us?

Teach me, O God, the compelling nature of your call, wherever and from whomever it sounds.

Encountering Jesus Today

Consider a duty you face this day or week whose value you wrestle with or whose doing repels you. Where in that action might there be an opportunity to be of service to others, a possibility of growth for you, a potential for encounter with God? Carry out that duty with these possibilities in mind and heart. See where it leads—and where it calls.

DAY FIVE

When I first sketched out this chapter on call, the story of the women at the tomb seemed a fitting conclusion. The Gospels' missional call to "go and tell" invests the women with the authority to be the first witnesses to Easter. In Matthew that call comes not once but twice: first from the angel at the tomb ("go quickly and tell his disciples") and then from the Risen Jesus ("go and tell my brothers"). Their call becomes the church's call to mission and witness, to go and tell in word and deed the gospel of resurrected life.

But then, the text interrupted my well-laid plans. You see, before the women (and we along with them) receive that commissioning call to "go and tell," the narrative relates another call. And without heeding this prior invitation, "go and tell" will never happen for them or for us.

"Come, see."

It is not the first time those verbs have been paired in a call story. Two followers of John the Baptizer ask Jesus where he is staying, and Jesus says: *Come and see* (John 1:39). A Samaritan woman Jesus spoke with at a well returns to her people and invites them to consider the possibility that Jesus is Messiah by saying: *Come and see* (John 4:29). In both cases, the words invite an experience of something or someone new. In both cases, the invitation to "come and see" intends to generate a personal decision about that new thing . . . or that new one.

So what call does "come and see" invoke for these women at the tomb? Remember, first, what they *had* come to see when this story began. "Mary Magdalene and the other Mary went to see the *tomb*" (emphasis added). When these women set out at the dawning of this day, they were likely on their way to prepare the corpse according to the traditions of their time. On a different level, they were on their way to see what can happen when you get in the way of the powers that be in this world. In either case, they were on their way to see the truth that all things end in death.

That way is interrupted. It is first interrupted by the pronouncement: "do not be afraid." Even so, the commission to be Easter apostles does not follow immediately. First, the women receive invitation to experience Easter's stunning reversal on a personal level. "Come, see." Before you can tell the news, you have to know the news. Before you can speak the truth, you have to experience the truth. Then and only then does the angel and then Jesus send the women on their way. Then, and only then, do they "go and tell"—because having come and seen, they are now in a position to speak out of their own experience.

The church sometimes neglects this sequence in its life. We are so eager to have folks busily engaged in the work of going and telling and doing that we fail to provide the needed preparatory time of experiencing grace and community. We rush to get new members connected through this committee or that task force as soon as possible, either in hopes of buoying up depleted ranks or in fear of losing the new ones out the back door. In some settings, folks are not even members when we sweep them into teaching Sunday school or serving on a mission board or . . . you get the picture. Perhaps you have even *been* the picture. We hurriedly involve people in calls and ministries, sometimes without allowing them to linger in the gift of *come and see*. How can we be spokespersons or exemplars of a faith that we have not taken the time to experience for ourselves?

It is important business, this coming and seeing. It is the equivalent of owning the faith rather than merely hearing about it. Consider the women at the tomb. *Come and see* was not merely an invitation to notice that a body was missing. *Come and see* was a call to trust that the powers of this world that brought about Jesus' execution did not possess the power and authority they claimed because they could wield death. *Come and see* was a call to hope that death is not the final word for us or for creation. *Come and see* provided the foundation for a faith and a witness able to defy those who stake their position on violence and death. Why? Because Easter bids us *come and see* for ourselves the death-defying-by-life-raising power of God.

Easter's call to *come and see* remains such a summons to the gracious possibility that life still speaks the final word and to make that word the basis for our life, our hope, our trust. Once we experience that word as personal truth, once we have come and seen the grace of God revealed in the raising of Jesus—then, like those women at the tomb, we have something to go and talk about, to go and live about, to go and serve about.

Then as now, owning the faith precedes its witness. Before our call to go out and make disciples of all nations, our preceding call is to *come and see* what being a disciple means. The season of Lent offers such a time and invitation. We follow Jesus on the way to Jerusalem and explore the stories of these individuals' contacts with Jesus so that we may come and see what such encounter means for us. For then, we will speak and act not solely out of the testimony of the church—but out of our own experience of the Crucified and Risen One.

Do not be afraid. Come and see.

Open me to see what you make possible, O God; and then, to live what you grace me to see.

Encountering Jesus Today

Where have you seen God's grace in your life? What have you experienced as Christ's love or Spirit's power in the midst of this world? Keep these in mind as opportunities arise to live out your faith. Let what you do (ministry) or say (witness) reflect what you have seen and experienced of God in your life and in this creation.

Week Two

CHALLENGED

CHALLENGES OF ALL SORTS confront us in life. Sports challenge our physical capabilities to strive beyond previous achievements of endurance or excellence. Work challenges our abilities to work alone or with others to achieve a task. Community challenges our commitment to live with and for others, some of whom we might be inclined to ignore or avoid. Lent challenges our faith to share the journey with Jesus toward Jerusalem, and then Golgotha.

The Gospels describe a variety of people whose encounters with Jesus result in challenge. In most instances, Jesus challenges those individuals themselves—and through them, us. Jesus encourages them, and us, to conceive of family and community beyond societal norms. Jesus confronts them, and us, to decide for ourselves whether Jesus' ministries of compassion and justice embody God's purposes for this world. Jesus calls them, and us, to a discipleship whose core is self-yielding service rather than self-serving privilege. At times, Jesus challenges others on behalf of the characters he encounters. When children are excluded, Jesus charges disciples and church to include and learn from the little ones among us. When an opponent suffers injury, Jesus' enjoins followers then and now to renounce violence.

Jesus' call, explored in the previous chapter, inevitably brings challenge. This chapter's readings tell of lives gospeled by such challenge. Lent invites us to consider and embrace their experiences as we travel on the way of the cross. Listen to these stories and hear the summons that encounter with Christ still brings to those who would follow on the Way.

DAY ONE

Mary and Jesus' Family   *Mark 3:19b-21, 31-35*

The term "family values" has become a lightning rod in our time. Opposing sides on arguments and divisions as varied as gay rights, welfare reform, and tax codes all claim that they are the ones who *truly* champion family values. The church has been drawn into those wider debates of society as well as into others more peculiar to life in the community of faith. Liberals and conservatives, evangelicals and charismatics, progressives and traditionalists: all regularly lobby their platforms and beliefs as representing the biblical core of family values.

Sometimes lost in these posturings are the biblical texts themselves, where families form the focus of living narratives rather than closed ideologies. Some of those texts affirm age-old principles of family. *Honor your father and mother. . . . Be subject to one another out of reverence for Christ. . . . Do not provoke your children to anger.* But when stories of actual families take center stage in the biblical narrative, family values become harder to see. Cain and Abel remind us family violence is not a modern-day devolution from idyllic beginnings, whether we locate the ideal in Genesis or the 1950s. Father Abraham, the exemplar of faith, twice passed off his wife as his sister out of fear. The Gospels mention Peter's mother-in-law—so why is Peter's wife totally off the New Testament's radar scope if families are of such high value? Above all else, perhaps no narrative challenges the relationship between faith and family more than the story of Jesus being sought by his mother and brothers and sisters.

According to Mark, the family seeks Jesus in order to "restrain" him. Rumors circulate that this, their son and brother, has lost his mind. Why? Jesus has broken the sabbath laws, at least in the view of some, and that breach has launched a plot to "destroy" him (3:1-6).

Whether *destroy* means reputation or life is not clear. What is clear is the family's move to rein him in. Families can be like that. They can rally around a threatened one, whether the threat comes from others or that individual's own bad choices. Family members may fight among themselves, but any outsider who enters the fray is liable to be set upon even by the ones they sought to support. Why? Families take care of their own.

The verb Mark uses for the family's action is stronger than its translation "restrain." The word can also mean "seize" or "control." If Jesus has gone out and gotten himself in trouble, which he has, the text suggests his family intends to get him back under control. The story reads like an ancient version of a family intervention for someone whose life has gotten out of kilter. The whole clan shows up: Mary, the brothers, and according to several ancient manuscripts, the sisters. The whole family intervenes with this child. They will take control of the situation by taking control of him. Family comes first, and the challenge they take on is to restore Jesus to family. But quite a different challenge comes their way, and our own.

It begins when the crowd surrounding Jesus leaves family on the outside looking in. All the family can do is send word to him. But the one they wait to bring home offers a word of his own, a word that may still shock as it did then. "Who are my mother and my brothers? . . . Here are my mother and my brothers!" Jesus was not looking at Mary and his family when he spoke. He was looking at the followers and the strangers, at the ones called and the ones simply curious, at the ones who came not to return him to an old life but to hear his words of a new life. "Whoever does the will of God is my brother and sister and mother."

Family values? Jesus leaves standing outside the woman who gave him birth, the siblings with whom he was raised—the very family from whom he learned the meaning and practice of love. Talk about challenges! Imagine yourself in the place of Mary or one of those siblings.

Then again, imagine yourself in the place of one of those gathered around Jesus whom he had just named as community, as family. Imagine yourself in the place of one of those who might otherwise have had no place. Jesus did, after all, have a reputation for spending time with folks least likely to receive Man or Woman of the Year recognition by the religious and community leaders of that day. Imagine yourself as one of those, now graced with a home. Or, imagine yourself in the place of those religious and community leaders who have witnessed the way Jesus leaves his own kin outside, and in the breach of sabbath leaves his own community behind. Would you put up with such change as Jesus teaches and practices?

That is the challenge Jesus brings: to view community and kinship in ways that turn long-standing traditions of relationship upside down. It is the challenge to experience community and kinship with those unrelated by blood, with those unrelated by commonalities of political persuasion or gender attractions or economic status. It is the challenge to affirm that community in Christ is founded solely on the grace of our being named by Jesus as brother and sister and mother, and our ensuing call to do the will of God as done by Jesus.

Mother and Father God, for the gift of family, whose kinship hears your grace and does your will: I give you thanks.

Encountering Jesus Today

Reread Mark 3:31-33. How does the passage challenge you: to be open to kinship with others in Christ; to give up seeking to "control" what Christ would or would not do in your life or community; to affirm what it means to do the will of God in the context of your life?

Day Two

John the Baptizer   *Matthew 11:2-6*

Death was near. It would be unnerving to come to the close of your days fearing that the vision and hope that had defined your life and vocation were an unfortunate misjudgment. So from a prison cell, from which he would not return, John dispatches disciples to ask Jesus *the* question.

"Are you the one?"

From time to time we may have raised similar questions in our lives. When a choice loomed between a current job, whose blessings and banes were at least known, and another that held both promise and uncertainty: which one would it be for you? When a relationship teetered between friendship and something far more serious: is this the one? Looking back on a life in which choices have been made, and joys and sorrows have resulted: does all this, in the end, make sense and hold together, or have I missed something from the very beginning?

"Are you the one?"

John's words to Jesus are challenging. They put the matter of whether Jesus offers fulfillment or disillusion squarely in the lap of Jesus, for him to say yes or no. But the challenge *to* Jesus swiftly becomes the challenge *from* Jesus. He does not tell John what to believe or not believe as to whether Jesus is the one. Rather, Jesus instructs the bearers of the question to go back and report what they have witnessed. Faith does not find resolution by putting Jesus' or God's back to the wall, and demanding an answer once and for all about whether we've all just been kidding ourselves with all this God talk. No, faith for us like faith for the Baptizer comes in having our ultimatums *to* the Holy turned into searchings *for* the Holy. Jesus bids us to discern in the sights and sounds of creation, in the experience of community, whether this God business is real or just pious blustering. What do *we* see and hear?

To be sure, Jesus highlights the sights and sounds available for those disciples of John to consider and pass on. The recitation more than coincidentally follows the hopes of Isaiah 61 about what God's coming might trigger. The blind go sighted. The immobile regain mobility. The ones not to be touched now find cleansing so that they may be embraced. The unhearing now listen. The dead are raised. And, perhaps in an ironic statement of something even more remarkable than resurrection—the poor get good news for a change. Can you believe that?

That is just the point. If John—or we—can believe that, the answer to "Are you the one?" will be obvious. Because such things do not happen by chance or coincidence. Such things happen when God comes among us.

Yet, as remarkable as healings and good news are, they still seem an odd way to answer someone who has spent his whole life preparing the way for Messiah. Jesus' words likely challenged John, for they do not appear to be in sync with the Messiah John had been proclaiming: the one who would come out with fire and judgment, the one who would put the axe to deadwood and burn the chaff. Jesus didn't point to a single act of brimstone preaching or enemy branding or evildoer banishing in response to "Are you the one?" No, the messianic actions Jesus pointed to involved healing and life-giving and offering the poor good news.

But lest we think old John a bit dense for having to ask the question, let's not forget the challenge of Jesus' words to us. We may not ask Jesus outright, "Are you the one?" Although occasionally, when things go haywire at church or in our personal lives or in the world at large, maybe we do indirectly. Maybe we imply "Are you the one?" when the question on our lips or minds is "Is this all there is?" Maybe we wonder "Are you the one?" when innocents perish or relationships unravel or health deteriorates, and all we can get out of mouths and spirits is "What's up with this?" For if Jesus *is* the one, then why all of this? Should we be looking for something or someone else?

Challenging questions, to be sure—as challenging as life itself. God in Christ is not offended or angered by our asking them, any more than Jesus was offended or angered by John's inquiry. God in Christ responds in turn with the summons to hear and see the answer for ourselves. To hear and see, in the most marginalized of places and persons, the signs of Messiah among us: in the restoration of wholeness, the renewal of life, and the gift of hope.

Do you hear and see such things? And if so, do you trust your life to the One who does them, who then bids you come and join him in Messiah's work? God does not tell you what your answer will be. The challenge of faith is to answer for yourself.

"Are you the one?" What say you?

You are the One, O Christ. So may I go and tell and live.

Encountering Jesus Today

Imagine yourself as one of the disciples sent back to John with Jesus' message. Imagine John replying to your litany: *That's well and good for Jesus to say, but just when and where did YOU see any of that?* How would you answer John? That is, have you witnessed sight restored, movement by those who were paralyzed in body or fear, outcasts brought back into community, listening by those who could not or would not hear, life brought out of death, or good brought to the poor? Would what you say be enough to convince *you*?

Day Three

James and John   *Mark 10:35-45*

When I neared the end of college, I received a cordial letter from the Standard Oil Corporation. Apparently I was just about their best friend in the world, a soon-to-be college graduate with a sterling earning potential. In gratitude for my friendship and in recognition of my Rockefeller-like future (Bill Gates hadn't come along yet), the company enclosed a 2 by 3 plastic rectangle embossed with my name. With it, I could drive to the nearest station and ask them to give me whatever I wanted, at least in the way of petroleum products. Soon, other oil companies saw me as their friend and extended the same offer. They were all more than eager to make my debt their acquaintance without ever having met this unemployed student.

At least James and John were known to Jesus. They had journeyed with him through Galilee, and now followed on the way that led to Jerusalem. Apparently, their experience with Jesus emboldened them to take a practical look at what was in this for them. Like my good friends at the oil companies, they settled on the equation of friendship, if not faith, as credit extension. "Teacher, we want you to do for us whatever we ask of you." When Jesus asked them to clarify what they wanted, their answer pinpointed the best seats in the house in God's realm. They wanted the places of privilege and power. The other disciples heard about this pre-emptive strike and got angry. The text is not clear, however, whether they were angry with these two for making such an outlandish request or for their asking first.

"We want you to do for us whatever we ask of you." The words sound strikingly modern in tone. They evoke the attitude of consumerism, synonymous with "what's in it for us." This approach to life transforms the political community. *Congress, we want you to do whatever we ask. Give us the finest health care system in the world accessible for all; underwrite education that will truly prepare our youth for the twenty-first century; protect us with the best armed services; keep our roads and highways patched and smooth; reclaim our cities and restore our environment; and, by the way, make sure the taxes to pay for this and all those other good things we've come to expect go down. Better yet, charge all this to our account—or more accurately, the account that will indenture our children and grandchildren to pay off our debt.*

This approach to life also transforms religious community. We want the church to do for us—and be for us—whatever we want. So congregations compete in trotting out the greatest number of programs to appeal to church shoppers, whose first concern is how this or that community meets their personal needs. We expect pastors to be gifted simultaneously in youth work and elder visitation, community involvement and financial administration and also invest long hours in the study to create compelling sermons that will draw new people in but not offend anyone except those we know shouldn't be in the church anyway.

"We want you to do for us whatever we ask" remains a formula for disaster. And it does not go unchallenged by Jesus. He begins by telling James and John such a request is not his to give. Not his to give? *Wait a minute*, we can hear the disciples protesting, *aren't you Messiah?* Think for a moment what Jesus implies. Even the Christ does not get to do whatever he wants. Even the Christ defers to the authority of God. The path of faith is not the exercise of personal prerogative. The true nature of that path is revealed in Jesus' challenge to the whole community that has been disrupted by this episode. Jesus challenges the church to have a view and practice of authority that is precisely opposite to the wider culture of that day and our own. "Lording it over" others is not how Christian community functions, no matter how efficiently it seems to work in the corporate world or political backrooms. Power and privilege reside in service. If you want to be first in line, you take care of all the others in line first.

So how do we, as individuals or communities of faith, find it possible to move away from the obsession with "we want you to do for us whatever we ask"? Listen again to Jesus' initial response to James and John. "What is it you want me to do for you?" On one level, the question simply asks for clarification. But more significantly, it is the hallmark of the kind of community and discipleship that Jesus challenges any prospective follower to adopt. It is the challenge to make Jesus' question, not the disciples' request, the basis of our walk with God.

"What is it you want me to do for you?" On our lips, that question changes relationship with God from bargaining for what I can get into offering what I have been given. On our lips, that question transforms our participation in Christian community from "shopping around" for the best deal into entering a covenant to live for the sake of Christ by living for the sake of others and all creation.

In my heart, through my life, within my church: what do you want me to do for you, O God?

Encountering Jesus Today

Consider a conflicted situation or dilemma you face. Bring that situation into mind as clearly as you can. Then, aloud or in silence, pray: *what is it you want me to do for you?* Do so several times, with silence in between for reflection and listening. Try to practice this prayer as a matter of first resort whenever you face a choice, an opportunity, or a challenge.

DAY FOUR

Children   *Mark 10:13-16*

Before we get all stirred up into righteous indignation about disciples who speak sternly to those wanting to bring children to Jesus, we need to remember a few things. We need to remember our impatience when a child cried or fidgeted in the sanctuary and interrupted our spiritual reveries. We need to remember how much money our congregation voted to put into the building maintenance fund this year and how much the church saved by making sure we kept spending for curricula and Christian education supplies to a minimum. We need to remember we did so as adults with responsibilities.

We need to remember these disciples of Jesus are no different from us. They know, as we do, there are priorities. Imagine their thoughts when the parade of runny-nosed toddlers and grimy-faced tykes starts closing ranks round the rabbi: *There are sermons to be preached. Diseased people to be cured. Didn't the Master speak of crosses to be carried? So much to do, so little time—go on, shoo! Don't bother the rabbi. He's too busy, too important! Shoo!!!*

The disciples have a point. After all, Mark declares that people brought these children for the sake of a mere touch. They didn't ask for a children's sermon or an object story to disguise this as a bona fide teaching moment. Just a simple touch. That's probably all the kids could understand anyway. And that's probably what got the disciples in a tizzy. You don't have to be God's gift to humanity to touch children. Anybody can do that. People with less important things to do can do that.

That rationale may explain, to some extent, why the church in years past begrudgingly agreed to ordain women, so long as they stuck to youth work and Christian education, the institutional equivalent of touching children. So long as they left the really *important* things, like preaching and presiding at council meetings, to the brethren. Anybody can touch children. So disciples of our day continue to mirror disciples of Jesus' day. Don't bother the rabbi! Don't interrupt Jesus' ministry. Shoo!

But as one of my preaching mentors once said, interruptions often *are* the ministry: the phone call in the midst of sermon preparation, the drop-in visit at the office, every disruption when matters important enough to block out time on the calendar collide with an unscheduled opportunity to touch another's life. Now here's the catch. Life and ministry don't work that way just for ordained ministers. God splatters *each* of our lives with unheralded yet opportune moments that come at us out of nowhere—and that disappear just as quickly. We're left to decide in that figurative or literal split second: what, and who, is more important.

Jesus' indignation toward the disciples arises from an unspoken but clear determination that these children are just as important as sermons and parables and Very Important Adults. He makes time and space for the little ones to come, remarking in the process that the disciples could learn a thing or two from children about God's sovereign realm. The same realm, it should be noted, of which Jesus had been laboring for nearly three years to offer them a glimpse that they still struggle to see in all their grown-upness. A glimpse is now provided, Jesus admonishes, in this unlikely herd of cooing infants and three-year-olds babbling on about their pet lamb or some such thing three-year-olds are apt to do.

"Let the little children come to me; do not stop them; for it is to such as these that the kingdom of God belongs." One wonders what would have happened to those children if Jesus had not paused to touch them that day. Would their souls have been consigned to eternal damnation? I seriously doubt it. Would they have suffered from never having experienced a touch from the hands that spun stars and raised mountains? Who knows? We find no testimonies in scripture or tradition from persons telling us their initiation into faith came from Jesus' touch that day.

Jesus' decision to gather these children appears to have been less for their lasting benefit and more for the benefit of those disciples—and us. In Christ's example, we are presented with a model for responding to the little ones today: whether they be little in age, little in prestige, little in power, or little in money. What do *we* do, whom do *we* choose when our busyness and notions of self-importance meet people typically belittled as interruptions? The text closes with Jesus' poignant embrace and blessing of the children. Mark uses a verb translated here as "took in his arms." Its Greek root refers to the bend in the arm created when one cradles or enfolds something—or someone. The verb occurs in only one other verse in the New Testament. In both places, Jesus is the one who embraces. In both cases, those embraced are little ones.

Jesus' challenge to us is simple: go and do likewise. For by embracing little ones, we find ourselves embraced in a kingdom formed by the bend in God's arm.

May I seek your hands and blessing, O God—that I might be your hands and blessing for others.

ENCOUNTERING JESUS TODAY

What do you learn of grace and God from a child? Do something today a child might do. Finger paint. Make up a story. As you do, consider what it means to receive God as a little child does. Do that activity (or spend that quiet time) with a child's eye view of God. Afterward, think of a child you can spend time with this week, time you might ordinarily have spent on a grown-up pursuit. Be open to what God may teach you through that child and that time.

Slave of the High Priest *Luke 22:47-51*

"I want the last face you see in this world to be the face of love, so you look at me when they do this thing. I'll be the face of love for you." The words come from *Dead Man Walking*, the story of Sister Helen Prejean's ministry to death row inmates. She speaks the words to a condemned, and clearly guilty, murderer who will soon be strapped onto a gurney and receive a lethal injection. The words embody *intercession*, a term whose Latin roots literally mean "to go between." Sister Helen stands between this man and death to provide him with one last (or is it first?) sight of love and grace.

In the garden of Gethsemane, the cover of night cloaks more threat than mere betrayal. The kiss of Judas that does violence to relationship is swiftly followed by the cut of a sword that does physical violence. The sword is not wielded by one of those who have come to seize Jesus but by one of the rabbi's followers. That rabbi had once counseled loving enemies and turning the cheek to one who would strike it. Judas's desertion of community is matched by this infidelity to the community's basis in love. According to the Gospel of John, Peter is the one who lashes out in contradiction to the way Jesus taught. The assertion that it is Peter who strikes out in violence should not surprise us. When Jesus earlier taught the way of this Messiah to be suffering and rejection, Peter took issue. That day's popular conception of Messiah called for a deliverer who was a warrior, not a casualty.

Even more telling than the disciple who lashes out with a sword is the person who gets injured. It is not Judas, the one whose kiss marked the target. It is not a chief priest or officer of the Temple, who for some time had apparently sought to bring Jesus to their version of justice. It is not one of the soldiers who accompanied the group in case of trouble—trained and armed to strike back. No, the victim of violence is identified as the slave of the high priest. A slave is someone who does not act independently but only under orders. It would be unusual to arm a slave, especially if armed men already were present. The victim of Peter's sword is, quite possibly, an unarmed man who had no choice about being there in the first place.

Isn't that how violence usually goes? The first to be its victims are those who are least culpable. Rogue nations are placed under sanctions by the "civilized" world—and who suffers first? Not the folks in high offices of government or the upper echelons of military chains of command. The first victims are the innocents: the children, the elderly, the ill. Targeted sanctions and smart bombs may be precise in terms of geographical location (or not)—but no microchip distinguishes the flesh and suffering of innocent from guilty. It has been that way since the violence in Gethsemane, and long before that if the truth be told.

But remember, this chapter's readings hinge on the challenges presented by encounters with Jesus. So how are lives, then and now, gospeled by the challenges Jesus issues in Gethsemane? Two challenges from Jesus—one spoken, one enacted—intend to change those who bear Christ's name. First Jesus rejects violence as the means to deal with conflict and confrontation. "No more of this!" he cries out after violence is tried. Love of enemies is hard to practice when weapons hold the day. But Jesus bids us here to something deeper than deciding whether to brandish arms in the face of enemies. The challenge is to reconstitute the way we think and speak and react to those with whom we are in conflict. He summons us to be more creative in facing opposition than resorting to character assassination and gossip that fights fire with fire and leaves us all with burns on our hands and spirits. The challenge is to reject policies and practices that promote or ignore violence not only in society but also in our families and neighborhoods. "No more of this!"

The other challenge Jesus presents in this encounter comes not in words but in his action of intercession. Jesus touches the wounded man's ear and heals him. In doing so, Christ invites us to intercede for victims of violence, to stand between them and their suffering and those who inflict it. The challenge is to provide, as Sister Helen did, a glimpse of the face of Christ. It is not enough to say we oppose violence, whether of the domestic or international variety. Christ embodies our call, as best we are able, to stand between victims and what has been perpetrated upon them.

As if that were not challenge enough, consider the one for whom Jesus intercedes—the slave. While the choice may not have been his to be there, this man had gone out to seize Jesus. Whether or not he understood the implications of his complicity, this individual took part in what would result in thorns pressed down and nails driven in and timbers lifted up. So what does Jesus, who later suffers that violence, do to one of its accomplices? He touches. He heals. He sets the stage for Golgotha's intercession: "Father, forgive them; for they do not know what they are doing" (Luke 23:34).

Can we, by the grace of God, be the face of Christ—not only to the innocent victims of violence but also to those who are its accomplices and even perpetrators?

Jesus, intercede for me: that I might see how I might intercede and be your face for others.

ENCOUNTERING JESUS TODAY

Consider a situation where you might intercede for another's sake. In doing so, how might you provide a glimpse of the face of Christ for that individual? Pray for guidance as to how you might intercede in a way that, in the spirit of this text, touches and heals.

Week Three

REJECTED

A CHILD WAITS while designated captains choose teams for kick-ball. One by one, others are chosen. Only at the end, when most or all have been selected, does a begrudging nod come that child's way. A marriage disintegrates when one partner decides he or she needs someone else. In each case, and others like them, the experience of rejection weighs someone down.

The theme and experience of rejection are closely associated with Lent. Rejection permeates Jesus' teachings of what awaits him in Jerusalem. Rejection marks the church's later interpretation of Jesus as the Suffering Servant envisioned by Isaiah 53:3 ("He was despised and *rejected*" [emphasis added]). But rejection for Jesus does not lie exclusively in those final days or in the church's hindsight. From the outset of his ministry, Jesus' message and person are turned down. The reasons for rejection vary, as we will see in the encounters this chapter explores. Some say no because Jesus does not fit into a mold fashioned by how things used to be. One turns away because Jesus asks too much. Others reject a way considered threatening to their position. Two others reject Jesus because he does not serve their self-interest of religious dabbling and political opportunism.

Faith does not come as a supernatural wave of the hand divorced from the exercise of our will. Lives may go ungospeled precisely because God invests us with freedom to follow or to reject. Encounters that end in rejection form this chapter's focus. Listen to these stories, and to their seasoning of the stakes of Lent. Faith and discipleship are not automatic for our journey. Then as now, we are free to choose. Then as now, we are free to reject.

Day One

Hometown Crowd   *Mark 6:1-6*

In practically every sport, conventional wisdom assumes you would always rather play at home. There is the advantage of not having to travel, much less stay overnight out of town. Another factor involves the psychological advantage of playing before fans who cheer you on and may take equal pride in disrupting the other team's concentration.

The flip side of home-field advantage is that the folks at home want a return on their support and adulation. Naturally, one of the returns they like is a winning team, but it isn't the only one. Brian Bosworth, one of the most gifted athletes the Seattle Seahawks ever drafted, violated one of the cardinal rules in sports: never run down the hometown crowd. Just as sure as the folks at home take care of their own, they also will pay back those they understand to be abusing the relationship.

When Jesus returned to the synagogue at Nazareth, his childhood home, he stood before a hometown crowd. No doubt great joy and pride welled up within the assembly. A young man reared in their village had gone out and, if the grapevine was to be trusted, made a name for himself. But not only for himself. In a day when family names were basically nonexistent, a person's hometown name often supplemented the given name. The rise to fame of someone from your own village brought honor to the whole community. The townspeople of Nazareth likely experienced such honor through Jesus of Nazareth.

Homecomings sometimes include an expectation for words to honor the folks back home for their part. And these were the folks who had nurtured Jesus, the one now ready to speak. Mark does not record his words or the scripture he used. According to Luke, Jesus read a passage from Isaiah associated with the promise of

God's Messiah. When he finished reading, according to Luke, Jesus said: "Today this scripture has been fulfilled in your hearing." Is Jesus suggesting that the figure and activity Isaiah had written about was to be discovered in the one sitting before them now? The same one who had lived among them all those years—the child who played, the youth who questioned, the young man who cut ties and set out on his own?

Mark records the crowd's first response: "Where did this man get all this?" Which is to say, *Doesn't he remember who he's talking to? We're the ones who taught him the Torah and showed him the way. Has he forgotten his roots? He's the village carpenter, for heaven's sake!*

The text winds down in an anticlimax. The lack of acceptance leads to Mark's observation that Jesus "could do no deed of power there . . . and he was amazed at their unbelief" (vv. 5-6). Unbelief can be utterly amazing at times. But perhaps it is most ironic when the one not believed is the very one for whom these same persons, years ago, probably held high hopes. Had Mark recorded the reactions of the hometown crowd, they would have likely focused on disappointment. *What's happened to your boy, Mary? What's become of that child we knew?*

In the end, the hometown crowd rejects Jesus. Or as Mark puts it, they "took offense" at him. That verb in Greek is *skandalizo*—the root of "scandalize." Why is Jesus a scandal to folks who once know him best? Apparently, he outgrew the mold into which they have him poured and prefigured. These protests about his being the carpenter, Mary's son, the brother of all those siblings all center on defining Jesus in terms exclusive to the past. At one time in Nazareth, those categories did sum up who Jesus was. But times, and identities, and with them, vocation, can change. The Nazarenes reject such change in the status quo concerning Jesus.

If the truth be told, the hometown folks' rejection of Jesus might just be because they fear the possibility of such change in themselves. Some communities, and some churches, never get past that fear. When individuals no longer fit into the slots where we place them, when ideas outgrow the confines of our thinking, when change threatens to force new ways of viewing others or ourselves, two options emerge. One option circles the wagons, raises the walls, and rejects any possibility that change in us or others could be good or even possible. Another option considers that maybe—just maybe—God calls us to be something and someone other than what has always been. Encounter with Jesus posed that choice in Nazareth. Encounter with Jesus poses that choice in your zip code, in the communities where you and others come to be known in ways confining or liberating—or more often, something of both.

For the folks of Nazareth, that choice provoked a scandal resulting in rejection. What will that choice provoke in you?

Help me, O God, to open myself to you in ways I had not assumed you might come or speak.

Encountering Jesus Today

Reflect on how familiarity with or longevity in the faith may pose trouble for you—and your congregation—by blocking openness to God's fresh ways of working. Consider one struggle you have today in reconciling the image of the God you grew up with and the God you encounter (or seek) now. How might this scripture passage speak to you in this struggle? Pray for the Spirit to open your faith to experiencing and serving God in ways you have not considered or practiced before.

Day Two

A Rich Young Man   *Matthew 19:16-22*

I have always been fascinated with the Olympics. Part of the allure has to do with the more exotic aspects of some competitions. I have never seen a luge or tossed a sixteen-pound hammer. Part of the appeal comes from the discipline required. For most Olympic competitors, the desire must be practically all-consuming. Everything else must become secondary to the effort needed to be one of the world's top athletes in an event. In such an endeavor, yielding to whatever is required to achieve such skill must be paramount. Now that may sound rather extreme—and it is. When you hear the stories about a barely adolescent gymnast leaving her family to live with coaches and other competitors for years; when you hear of athletes who put in six hours of training per day, six days per week, fifty-two weeks per year: the "dream" begins to sound more like an obsession. Yet, in a way at once curious and unsettling, the single-minded passion of would-be Olympians touches on the nature of Christian discipleship. Perhaps no story reveals that kinship more clearly than Jesus' encounter with a rich young man.

This individual seeks Jesus out for advice. "What good deed must I do to have eternal life?" The question goes to the heart of all religious searching: what do I have to do? Jesus' initial response touches on deeds identified by Jewish tradition. What is intriguing here are the commandments Jesus names—and those he omits. He singles out those that govern relationship with others. He omits ones that deal with relationship with God. Conventional wisdom might have made first if not exclusive appeal to one's relationship to God. Jesus, however, teaches that the roots of eternal life are grounded in the soil of this life. We cannot ignore other people with the excuse of devoting attention to God in the quest for the eternal.

The young man's confident assertion that "I have kept all these" is qualified by his own recognition that something is still lacking. Ironically, Jesus identifies that lack with what this individual possesses in abundance. "Sell your possessions, and give the money to the poor. . . . then come, follow me." At that, the young man walks away, grieving. The desire that drove his pursuit of eternal life in the question "what must I do?" proves secondary to maintaining what he has already accumulated and accomplished. The story suggests ultimate values are revealed not so much in what we seek but more clearly in what we will not give up.

Making the transition from this individual's encounter with Jesus to our own hinges on understanding the story's focus on the single-minded nature of discipleship. This encounter *does not* create a universal call for financial divestment or self-impoverishment. The encounter *does* challenge us to make everything else secondary to pursuit of life connected to God. We are to do so in a way that honors Jesus' surprising revelation that life with God largely concerns the implications of loving our neighbor.

"What must I do?" The answer we hear in this encounter with Jesus compels us to consider what we would have greatest difficulty giving up in our own lives, even for the sake of God. For some of us, like this young man, the power of possessions to possess us may well be the issue. For others, the stumbling block may be found in other allegiances—even allegiances otherwise seen as good: love of nation, devotion to family. Anything we value more, and particularly anything we say we will never give up, stands as a potential rival to our seeking life with God. The story challenges us to ask ourselves if there is anything we could not set aside for the sake of relationship with God. Is there anything that would cause us to turn and walk away from Jesus, grieving?

Therein lies the power of this story to invite decision, yet not coerce it. Jesus does not make it impossible for this young man to reject Jesus' answer to the question of "what must I do?" The same is true for us. Grace would not be grace if we could not say no, if we could not choose to hold other allegiances higher, other commitments stronger, than seeking God. On the other hand, grace would not be grace if the demand were cheapened and discipleship depreciated into a negotiated settlement. Life with God is not a bargain to be argued down to the lowest common denominator. It is an all-consuming goal. It is a passion intended to shape how we conduct our relationships and the whole of our lives. Discipleship does not reject the rest of life: its beauties, its experiences, its companions. Discipleship restructures all in relationship to the One who gives meaning and hope to it all.

"What must I do?" The choice is ours, as it was for this young man, for what we will prize and value—and follow—above all else.

Holy One, giver of manna and grace for life, may I find in you all I need, that I may be truly free to live with and for others.

ENCOUNTERING JESUS TODAY

List on paper ten relationships and/or things that matter most in your life. Rank the list from highest (1) to lowest (10). Alongside the top two or three, note why each holds such importance in your life. Of those top three, what in them might stand in the way of relationship with God? Consider how faith might shape those priorities—not removing them from your life but transforming them into expressions of rather than hurdles to following Jesus.

DAY THREE

Leaders   Mark 3:1-6

Politics makes strange bedfellows, the saying goes. So does religion—or to be more precise in terms of Mark's story, so does opposition to Jesus' interpretation of sabbath. The text singles out two otherwise estranged groups united by such opposition: Pharisees and Herodians.

Pharisees served as leaders for those who viewed the heart of Judaism to be faithful adherence to the Jewish law or Torah. During and since the time of exile, sabbath keeping emerged as central to both Torah observance and Jewish identity. The Pharisees were not some fringe group in Judaism, religious extremists akin to the political fanatics who came to be known as Zealots. The Gospels sometimes overstate the conflict between Jesus and the Pharisees. Some scholars argue that with the destruction of the Temple by Rome in 70 CE, the core of Jewish identity shifted from the temple to the synagogue. With the Zealots defeated, the Herodians deposed, and the Sadducees without a temple to administer, Judaism largely followed the Pharisaic path. When the early church and Judaism began to take increasingly separate paths, the church (and the writers of the New Testament materials) sought to trace their differences with Pharisaic Judaism to Jesus' relationships with the Pharisees.

The truth is, Jesus and the Pharisees were not that far apart. The Pharisee Nicodemus declared to Jesus that "*we* know that you are a teacher who has come from God." Other Pharisees warned Jesus of the danger posed to him by Herod Antipas (Luke 13:31). Jesus kept table fellowship with Pharisees in a story we will look at in this book's final chapter. Jesus' teachings about keeping the law in the Sermon on the Mount (Matt. 5:17-20) reflect the essence of the Pharisees' teachings. Yet Pharisees—clearly some but definitely not all—reject Jesus early on.

Mark identifies those with whom these particular Pharisees conspire as "Herodians."

Who are the Herodians? To translate their standing into today's terms, Herodians would be the people whose pictures appear on the newspaper society pages. Herodians would have seats on the dais when the president gives a speech or the CEO addresses a conference. In other words, Herodians represent the establishment: political, social, religious. Herodians are the moneyed, the powerful, the movers and shakers. In Jesus' day Herodians were less of a party, in the sense of the Pharisees, as they were an unofficial designation for the privileged class. They took their name from the ruling family sired by Herod the Great, whose son Herod Antipas ruled the territories of Perea (where John the Baptizer ministered) and Galilee (where Jesus' public ministry began).

The pairing of Pharisees and Herodians seems like a match made anywhere but in heaven. At best, Herodians paid lip service to Torah observance. The law certainly did not restrain their titular head, Herod Antipas, from marrying a woman who was both his niece and sister-in-law. But like the elite of any day, their overriding goal was to maintain the status quo, seeing as how they balanced on top of that heap. Any unrest, civil or religious, would not be appreciated. The perceived undermining of a bedrock societal foundation like sabbath keeping would have been most unwelcome. As a result, an unspecified number of Pharisees and Herodians conspire to destroy Jesus. Their collusion is mere prelude to the later collusion by temple authorities and Roman leaders that eventuates in Jesus' crucifixion.

This encounter that unleashes rejection by some religious and civil leaders of Jesus' day merits caution in our own. Keep in mind what evoked their rejection: an innovation in established tradition by Jesus. We miss the point of this encounter if we say that since we no longer have the same scruples about observing sabbath, that this story is just about an ancient Jewish issue. Friends, it is a

Christian problem too. Innovation in tradition can be a problem for *any* religious tradition, especially those where the lines between religious and civil authorities blur. Rejection came then because Jesus rocked the boat. Rejection still is apt to come now when we open our lives and churches to something more than a "gentle Jesus meek and mild."

Remember the story itself: the scene and the silence around him provoked Jesus' anger. Imagine today the scenes that probably provoke Jesus' anger: millions of children dying each year from hunger and lack of medicine simply by virtue of their birthplace; obscene disparities in wages between workers and executives; the violence of terror—and the violence of states—against innocents. Imagine—although it really doesn't take much imagination—the silence that accepts such realities, either out of resignation or self-interest.

What would happen if individuals and communities of faith today translated righteous indignation into righteous action against such scenes and in the face of such silence, as did Jesus? No doubt, strange bedfellows inside and outside the church would again band together to oppose such tampering with tradition. They and others would say, "Don't rock the boat."

And a few, including Jesus, I suspect, would say to the disturbers of such uneasy peace, "Well done, good and faithful servants, well done."

Remind me, O God, there is no law against doing good, no matter the situation or opposition.

Encountering Jesus Today

What scene comes to your mind that would provoke Jesus' anger, where fear or indifference blocks the doing of good? Decide on one action, however small, you will take this day to do the good you envision Christ would do if he were in your shoes. As you take that action, keep in mind that Christ is in your shoes and in your doing of the good.

DAY FOUR

Herod Antipas Luke 23:6-12

To dabble: to undertake something superficially or without serious intent. Most of us dabble at an endeavor from time to time. I used to dabble at stone polishing. I purchased rock tumblers and the various grits used for each stage of the process. I polished batches of rocks for a couple of years. But over time, I lost interest. I could take it or leave it, and I pretty much left it. I suppose hobbies could be considered forms of dabbling, although hobbies generally involve a level of self-investment. To dabble is more like flitting from one bright shiny object to the next one, without any desire to go beneath the surface. When we dabble, we spend time on something that really does not affect or change us.

Enter Herod Antipas, dabbler extraordinaire. At least, that is the impression we derive from this narrative. Certainly the musical *Jesus Christ Superstar* portrays him that way. In that stage production Herod Antipas comes across as a malevolent fop whose only interest in Jesus is to gain a momentary rush of spiritual excitement. At Jesus' trial before Herod, the king expectantly (or is it mockingly?) sings: "Prove to me that you're no fool, walk across my swimming pool."

The Gospels do not record so crass a statement. But almost. Luke alone records this episode when Jesus' trial before Pilate is interrupted by the appearance before Herod. For a moment, it appears the ominous turn of events after arrest in the garden has taken a more fortunate direction for Jesus. Luke notes Herod was glad to see Jesus. In fact, Herod had wanted to see him for some time. But Herod's rejoicing had nothing to do with any desire to learn from the rabbi. Rather, Herod "was hoping to see him perform some sign." Do something, Jesus. Heal a leper. Swallow a goldfish. Show me a God trick.

Signs are a curious thing in the New Testament. By their very nature, they are intended to be transparent—that is, to help persons see through them into the saving activity and presence of God at work in Jesus. But for some, the signs themselves become all that is sought. The sign of the loaves and fishes in John's Gospel turned the crowd into would-be kingmakers. After all, put Jesus in a position of power, and just imagine what else he could do for us! So it is not surprising that Jesus himself comes to take a somewhat jaded view of signs, and those whose religious quest seems to be limited to seeking after them. Jesus flees from those who seek signs in order to test him (Mark 8:11-13). In Luke 11, Jesus implicitly links this seeking of signs with a generation he describes as "evil." And now, Jesus finds himself confronted by Herod, the dabbler in things spiritual, who would like Jesus to charge his batteries with some spiritual magic.

The fact that the encounter quickly sours ought not to surprise. Herod the dabbler has no time to waste on things or persons that do not please or excite. His earlier dabbling with John the Baptizer had come to a screeching halt when his libido ran ahead of his infatuation with John's righteousness. A young woman's dance got Herod's attention, and lost John his head. So now, when Jesus offers no word much less any miracle to pique his curiosity, Herod loses interest. Time to move on to the next passing fancy. He sends Jesus back to Pilate. Bring on the next act. It is almost unfair to list Herod among those who reject Jesus. Rejection implies a degree of seriousness about weighing a choice—and dabbling by nature avoids seriousness. On the other hand, Herod's story provides a timely reminder to individuals and communities today: dabbling has nothing to do with discipleship.

Religious dabbling is alive and well among us. Some forms of church shopping today are little more than "dabbling" at discipleship. *Let's see what this church can do for me and mine* is not all that far removed from *let's see whether Jesus will perform a sign for me.*

Perhaps even more critical, some forms of faith involvement are little more than "dabbling" at discipleship. As long as we don't scratch beneath the surface of my life or the status quo around here, as long as all this "religious" stuff is not taken too seriously: everything will be alright.

But will it? And will we?

Dabbling is all about keeping things on the surface. Discipleship goes deep into our world and into us. Dabbling is all about the momentary piquing of our curiosity before we move on to the next oddity that attracts—or distracts—our attention. Discipleship is all about fidelity that keeps faith with One whose presence is steady and whose call is demanding. Dabbling leaves us unaffected. Discipleship intends to change us at the core. Dabbling naturally leads to mocking the committed. Discipleship inevitably calls to living committed.

Which will it be for us?

May I be glad to see you, God—and may I be gladder still to follow you on the Way.

ENCOUNTERING JESUS TODAY

Identify one place in your spiritual journey where you may be just "dabbling"—dealing with things on the surface, going through the motions. It may be in your prayer life, your ministry to others, or your ethical conduct. What might a transition from dabbling to discipleship look like in that one area? Commit yourself to one practical action you will take this week, or even today, that begins to move this dimension of your spiritual journey beyond the superficial.

Day Five

Pilate   *Mark 15:1-15*

My baptism in political campaigns—and political expediencies—came in the summer of 1972 when I volunteered to work for George McGovern's campaign. I spent several days manning a phone bank in a St. Louis location I have long since forgotten. What I do remember clearly was my departure from the campaign. Senator Thomas Eagleton of Missouri had been chosen as McGovern's running mate, a partnership that lasted slightly more than two weeks. Then, information surfaced that Eagleton had electroshock treatments for depression six years previous, a fact not divulged to his presidential running partner. McGovern at first came out fully supportive of Eagleton, saying he would back him 1,000 percent. He even joked that he himself would undergo psychiatric evaluation as long as his Republican opponent Richard Nixon would as well. But three days later, McGovern himself asked Eagleton to resign, and Eagleton did. The intervening tar-and-feathering of a fellow Missourian, coupled with the awkward turnaround by McGovern, sealed the deal for my departure from the campaign. It also reinforced my understanding of how political expediency can run roughshod over those who stand in its way.

I say "reinforced" in the previous sentence because of my Sunday school teachers and pastors at Salvator Evangelical and Reformed Church. Not that they were political activists by any means. More importantly, at least in terms of my formation, they were the ones who told me stories. They told me the story of David and Uriah. They told me the story of Esther. They told me the story of Daniel. And they told me the story of Pilate.

They told me the story about Pilate's finding no case against Jesus in an attempt to foist the decision to execute him on others. Then Pilate made an offer to release a prisoner, seemingly in hopes of releasing Jesus. When that failed, my teachers told me, Pilate washed his hands, as if water and a bit of soap could scrub off innocent blood. When that failed, they told me, Jesus was crucified.

Two things are important to keep in mind here. First, some take the Gospel accounts as portraying Pilate as almost a tragic figure, who cannot hold back the killing intent of some Jewish leaders. Let us be clear that outside of the biblical text, Pilate is portrayed in far less sympathetic terms. He flaunts Jewish piety by marching the Roman imperial standards into Jerusalem. He orders the massacre of a group of leading Samaritan citizens. It may be that the Gospel writers portray Pilate as they do in an effort not to upset the Roman rulers under whom their communities then currently lived.

Secondly, consider again the litany of Pilate stories I heard from my teachers and pastors. It is no coincidence that "when that failed" is a frequent refrain. Whatever role we assign to or remove from the group of Jewish leaders who conspired, whatever sympathies we might hold or withhold regarding Pilate's position: make no mistake. In every action and inaction of his, Pilate fails. And Pilate's failures result, as in most cases when expediency rather than justice rules the day, in the suffering of the innocent. At the end of the day, Jesus dies: not at the hands of Judas, not at the hands of some unknown number of Jewish conspirators, not at the edict of the Sanhedrin, not at the will of the Jewish people. Jesus does not even die so much at the hands of those who drive in the nails and lift up the timbers—for on their own and without orders, they could and would do nothing. Jesus dies at the hands of Pilate for the sake of political expediency. Or as Mark puts it, he dies because Pilate wished "to satisfy the crowd."

Rejection is a form of death. Rejection puts to death possibilities by closing doors to ideas or options, individuals or groups. Pilate's rejection of Jesus takes the matter to its logical albeit extreme end. Expediency understands it is better to reject one than to suffer rejection by the many. Better to satisfy the crowd than dare to stand against it. How many times have you heard that, how many times have you *seen* that, in your time?

The expedient rejection of Jesus by Pilate challenges us to consider the role expediency plays in our lives, our decisions, our relationships . . . and our spirituality. When we confront some difficult crossroad, when we face a possible hostile response to our values or choices: do we opt for expediency? Do we follow the example of water, and take the path of least resistance? Do we follow Pilate's example of a bowl of water, and try abdication of our responsibilities?

The path followed by Jesus and those who would follow him is rarely an expedient one. Its steps are not taken by premeditated measures of what best serves self-interest. Its steps are taken by what best serves God and others. Its love is not based on reciprocity, but on the gracious experience of being loved and loving graciously in return. Expediency abdicates more than responsibility—it abdicates opportunity. So it was for Pilate. So it remains for us.

Save me, O God, from acting to satisfy others—unless such actions satisfy your good.

Encountering Jesus Today

Consider when faith has not been "expedient" for you—and consider too when expediency managed to trump faithfulness. What are you too prone to try and "satisfy"? Be mindful of a place in your life today where that tendency is a real concern. Prayerfully seek God's leading to understand what it might mean to set aside expedience in that issue and replace it with integrity.

TRANSFORMED

THE HEBREW TRADITIONS of Jubilee called for a transformation of society every fiftieth year. The indebted and enslaved were to be freed. Lands lost were to be restored to the original family of ownership. Unfortunately, no record indicates Jubilee was ever kept. Perhaps that reality prompted Isaiah to cast the future's messianic hopes in the language of Jubilee: the Spirit-ed one who proclaimed the good news of God's year of favor would finally free captives, bind up the broken, and comfort the grieving (Isa. 61:1-3).

Luke records Isaiah's vision of Jubilee to be the commissioning text for Jesus' ministry (Luke 4:17-21). Isaiah's Jubilee anticipations unfold in the Gospels' stories of transforming encounter with Jesus. A body bent over to the point of breaking becomes straight. One without place in community has place restored. Another finds her desperation met, not with rejection and judgment, but with healing and peace. A mourning mother receives her son back while a mourning community moves from lament to praise. The One who comes to bring transformation finds transformation himself through the persistent faith of a Canaanite woman.

Encounter with Jesus, then as now, seeks life's transformation for the good. The path to such transformation, like the path of Lent, is not without difficulty or disruption. The status quo for others and us does not always go gentle into that good night when it comes to change. Attend to these characters, whose encounters with Jesus result in transformation—and listen for where they whisper the hope and promise of change on our own way toward Jerusalem.

67

DAY ONE

One thing leads to another. A sabbath. A stoop. A look. A hand. A healing. A praise. A complaint. A new sabbath. But we are getting ahead of ourselves. The details invite us to linger in this story and learn of transformation rippling outward from the one to the many.

The day is sabbath. Its keeping meant to transform Israel from a people defined by what they produced to a covenanted community claimed by the One who rested on creation's seventh day. That sabbath keeping came in the laws linked to the story of deliverance from Egypt is no coincidence. A people stooped over from hard labor and no hope received sabbath as a gift to observe God's own restful delight in creation—and in the process, to open its observers to the ongoing hope of sabbath's weekly ritual and promise of new creation.

So into Luke's story set on sabbath comes a woman stooped and bent under the weight of another sort of oppression. The detail that this woman has been so affected for eighteen years implies she had not been so from birth. There had been a time, it would seem, whether only as a child or into her adulthood, when her body did not twist downward. Once, apparently, she had been able to look into the sky or another's eyes without having to contort herself. But one thing for her likely led to another. A time of standing straight followed by a slight hunch, then a pronounced bend, until finally she is, in the literal words of the Greek text, "stooped together."

Eighteen years is a long time to live at such an angle. Eighteen years in our time marks the progress of infant to high school senior. What if that child never knew what it meant to stand straight, or had never in her life looked without great difficulty at anything other than the ground? We ought not pass by this detail of this woman's life as if it were unimportant. The time it takes for our children to grow up is the time she had been bound to grow down.

In Luke's story, as deformation gives way to transformation, one thing leads to another. It all begins when Jesus sees her. It can be easy to look away from what—or who—does not seem right in our view of how things should be. "Overlook" gets its name for a reason. If we do not wish to be troubled by the sights around us, we look elsewhere. We avoid the glance of the panhandler on the street. We switch channels when the news clips from Iraq or Darfur come on. But seeing is not just a physical attribute. It can be a spiritual discipline. Jesus' seeing of this woman opens his hands-on act of healing her. Transformation occurs when sight comes matched with word and touch. Then, and only then, does this woman stand up straight and praise God: one, and perhaps two, things that had escaped her for eighteen years.

One thing still leads to another. The act does not fit, in the sight of one religious leader, with the core value of sabbath keeping. Some interpreters pose the story from this point forward as Jesus in opposition or succession to Judaism—Jesus the transformer of Judaism into Christianity. Nothing of the sort occurs here. The foe is not first-century Judaism. The foe is any-century religious legalism. Jesus does not identify her as a daughter of the church. She is, by the grace of God and the witness of the text, a daughter of Abraham. Such grace energized by Jesus' sight and embodied by Jesus' words and hands frees her. And that grace incarnate in a sabbath cure frees sabbath from miniscule rules to matters of life and renewal. In other words, Jesus restores sabbath to its very Jewish origins and practices.

Does one thing still lead to another? Does transformation still come to ones bent over? In doing so, does transformation still come for traditions that stoop under the weight of so much legalism and self-righteous baggage that we fail to remember their original purposes and Spirit?

The story of this woman's transformation, and with it sabbath's transformation, reminds us to be on the watch—and on the practice—of one thing leading to others. How we look at others, or not, may set the stage for whether transformation will face an open or closed door in our lives. How we view and practice religious tradition, whether in opposition to or advocates on behalf of the human spirit fashioned in the divine image, may reveal whether transformation flows through or in spite of that tradition.

The dispute over sabbath's meaning looses ominous hints in the context of Lent. Legalists then and now do not take lightly the valuing of spirit over law. Sabbath breaking will become a key accusation leveled against Jesus. Transformation inevitably comes at great risk—because transformation has a way of one thing leading to another. The restoration of this one woman leads to the restoration of sabbath for all Israel; even as, in the gospel's ultimate promise of one thing leading to another, the raising of one pledges the raising of all.

Free me and straighten me, O God, to live in praise of you and in service of others.

ENCOUNTERING JESUS TODAY

How do you resemble the woman at the beginning of this story? In what places in your life are you "bent over" and "unable to stand straight"? Reflect on how and why Christ might seek your transformation. What might be "one thing leading to another" for your transformation?

Prayerfully seek God's leading in steps you might take on that path, even as you seek God's grace in changing what seems beyond your abilities at this moment. Trust that God seeks your good.

Day Two

Leper   *Matthew 8:1-4*

An instructor in preaching at my seminary was fond of talking about sermons in the words of a then-current slogan for tires: "where the rubber meets the road." That is, sermons are where ideas born of theology and scripture come into contact (or not) with our lives in the most pressing and practical of terms.

In the story at hand, a leper challenges Jesus that "if you choose, you can make me clean." Jesus replies, "I do choose. Be made clean." And he is. The miraculous transformation is neat and swift: one moment leprous, the next moment whole. But lest this be heard too casually, please know I first wrote this barely two days after I learned that one of my best friends from childhood was diagnosed with glioblastoma, an aggressive form of brain tumor. Current statistics suggest that only one out of four so stricken manage to survive even two years. The text in Matthew says: "If you choose you can make me clean. . . . I do choose." So forgive me if I wonder where the rubber of those words meets the road my friend now travels.

Some might say: God does choose healing, so if your friend *really* trusted God's choice of good health for him he would be made whole. I have two reactions to such theology. One involves an explicit Anglo-Saxon verb mingled with what anyone who has ever worked around a cow barn will be familiar with. My other reaction involves the truth that Jesus' healings in the New Testament do not always depend on the faith of the recipient. Sometimes, Jesus just does it. And I am glad Jesus does. Otherwise, we would be left with blaming folks who do not get well. It is the same twisted logic that argues some people are poor because they do not claim the prosperity Jesus wants them to have. I just wonder what such folks do when markets crash or when moth and rust (not to mention pension fund mangers and golden-parachuted

CEOs) doth corrupt. I most especially wonder what such folks think when they get their own terminal diagnosis—as we all eventually will. Healings do not always come.

So what, then, does this narrative mean when it speaks of Jesus' "choosing" of wholeness and the transformation it brings for this leper? Is this leper just an exceptional case, who happens to be in the right place at the right time? Or is there some fundamental assertion made here about transformation that goes beyond whether one individual gets a free pass to health and community, remembering leprosy resulted in ostracism, while many others then and now do not?

We tread on ground here that goes by the well-deserved name of mystery. Those who say they perfectly understand such things either do not see the whole picture, or they live a very sheltered life and faith that will one day collide with their own and their loved ones' mortality.

The ability to live faithfully in this mystery between "I do choose" and our experiences where such choices seem absent ultimately depends upon one's view of time. Faith lives in a tension between the world as it is and the world as it is promised. Previous eras swung too far in the direction of the otherworldly, urging the faith of European serfs or African American slaves to accept the brutalized conditions under which they lived in light of the Promised Land beyond the Jordan. Conditions as they existed were deemed "God's will," largely by folks who were not serfs or slaves. What was lost in such eras was the centrality of Jesus' incarnation and his ministry to the poor and hurting of this world. But it must also be avowed that the pendulum can swing too far in the other direction. The promises of faith and God's envisioned realm do not exhaust themselves in what occurs between our birthings and our dyings. What can become lost then is the love and justice of God that transcend those markers of our lives. Resurrection faith proclaims God's actions and our hopes are not limited to the interval between cradle and grave.

I do not pretend that this solves the mystery implicit in what

God chooses and what comes to pass—at least in our immediate experience. The wider perspective of time beyond cradle and grave does not absolve us from doing everything we can within those times to work for healing and transformation. Indeed, faithful prayer may well invoke and call to remembrance what God chooses for those whose lives hang in the balance. For sometimes, beyond our ken, healing does come and life in this sphere goes transformed.

But even when it does not, we stake our claims on the One who says "I do choose," trusting—not knowing, but trusting—that God will be faithful to God's word.

Since writing the first draft of this reading, I presided at the memorial service for my friend Randy. I do not believe that Jesus' "I do choose" means either that Jesus' word is not good or much less that God chose glioblastoma for Randy. I still trust, without understanding at the moment how, that the word of "I do choose" for wholeness will be kept. Not in my time. Certainly not by virtue of anything I can do. But until then, I will still pray for healing and wholeness to come now. Until then, we may all pray for those for whom God's choosing of wholeness seems in greatest peril and in most pressing need. In the incarnation, God in Christ has stamped these days with the promise of holy presence and possibility. In the resurrection, God in Christ has given second wind to prayers that have not gone answered as we hoped and to those who have not been healed as we sought—and to a realm that, while long deferred, will bring holy purposes to chosen fulfillment.

So help us, God.

May your good choices come in time, O God, and may we work and pray for their coming.

Encountering Jesus Today

Where do God's choices for wholeness seem painfully unfulfilled for a friend or loved one? Prayerfully consider what you can do in support and advocacy for that other. Then—do it.

Day Three

Woman with Hemorrhage   *Luke 8:43-48*

There are places and times when it seems we have reached our wit's end. Such times often bring a decisive moment. Having reached that end, we may despair and give up. Suicide, depression, and addiction reflect that option. We do not want the pain anymore, and anything that takes it away by taking *us* away becomes fair game. On the other hand, having reached that end, we may also do something in desperation we have never considered. Not long ago, a father in Canada, driven to the edge by his daughter's descent into an abusive and addictive relationship, shot and killed the young man he considered to be destroying her life and spirit. More than one individual in the last stages of cancer has made a trip to Lourdes or elsewhere in hope of a last-minute reprieve. Desperation can become a powerful liberator, whether from reason or faith or inhibition.

We ought not underplay the influence of desperation in Luke's story of this woman who seeks to touch the robe of Jesus. The desperation is present in the story's details. Her condition has persisted twelve years. Have you ever had a headache linger for days, or a cold hang on for weeks? Have you ever felt so sick after several hours of nausea that there seemed no end in sight? Insert the period of twelve years into any of the above conditions. What would you be willing to do at that point? The nature of this woman's condition also looms large in ascribing desperation her actions. While Luke does not provide an exact name to her disease, the words literally mean "flow of blood." The regulations of Leviticus 15:25-31 assert such a condition results in ritual uncleanness, which made her an outsider in her own community. She could not go to the Temple or attend the functions of the synagogue. Beyond that, anyone who even came into contact with her could be judged unclean as well.

The woman's desperation leads to action that jeopardizes herself and others. She risks public censure by coming into contact with anyone in the crowd. She risks making Jesus unclean. Hers is the desperation of one who will do anything to be healed, even if it means putting faith in touching a holy man's clothing.

To sensible ears, her act is ludicrous. To pious faith, her act seems far too close to magic for comfort. But sensibility and piety sometimes presume a world that is always and everywhere fair and equitable. When matters grow desperate, sensibility and piety sometimes come up short. For that reason, this woman's healing becomes an act of grace not only for her but all the rest of us who sometimes find ourselves overwhelmed with desperation.

You see, when this woman grasps for straws by grasping for the fringe of Jesus' cloak, something happens. Before Jesus turns and speaks, she experiences what she believes to be healing. And Jesus, when he does react, is gracious. He does not berate her for doing what could make him unclean. He does not scold her for such simplistic faith, if you could even call it faith, the notion that touching somebody's clothes could help you. He does not tell her to wait and come back when her beliefs are more mature and fitting with a selfless devotion to the One she seeks. No—Jesus accepts her for who and where she is. He commends the faith she does have, rather than pointing out where it may be lacking or immature. He offers peace, no small gift for someone who has known twelve years of anything *but* a peaceful existence. Your faith, Jesus says, has "made you well"—a word that elsewhere is translated as "saved." She goes her way transformed.

The transformation this woman experiences here is a gracious one. And her story of encounter spills into our own. Her experience brings hope to all the rest of us, that our need of change and welcome and healing by God in Christ does not have to wait until we have this faith thing all wrapped up in a tidy package. This is not a story that encourages us to place faith in objects. It is a story

that relates God's openness to those among us who are desperate—
which would mean, at one time or another, all of us. And when do
we most need the healing and transforming presence of God, if it
is not in our desperate times?

In her desperation, this woman does not give up but reaches
out for transformation. In our desperation, may we be willing to
risk doing the same. May we seek God in our desperate moments
as surely, if not as calmly, as we do when the sailing is smooth and
all is well. And may we find, in times of confusion and anxiety, the
peace and grace that transform us.

*God, whose mercy welcomes our grasping, may I seek you as did
this woman—without reserve, in hope, for the sake of transformation.*

Encountering Jesus Today

Where in your life are you in or near a place of desperation?
Prayerfully consider what it would mean to open your life to God's
transformation in that place. Be open to those possibilities even,
and especially, if you cannot at the moment precisely see the way
through. Seek out a mentor, a companion, or a small group whom
you trust: someone through whom God might work to bring peace
into your life. Be open, at this time or later, to serving in that role
for another who passes through desperate times.

Widow of Nain   *Luke 7:11-17*

More times than I care to remember I have officiated at rites where parents grieved the death of a child. It does not matter what euphemism we cast over that palled occasion: "funeral," "memorial," "celebration of life." In the end, it comes down to facing the awful truth that you have outlived your child. There is no easy way to do that. Maybe that is why we have no word in English to describe it. We have *widow* or *widower* to designate the loss of partner. We have *orphan* to denote one who has lost parents. But who are you when you lose your child?

Imagine this burial procession out of the village of Nain. As you do so, listen for the deep emotion just beneath the surface of Luke's words: "he was his mother's only son, and she was a widow." The words are far less about the deceased and far more about this woman: widowed *and* bereft of child. I have been told that the loss of a child is even more difficult than the loss of a partner. I have never had to cross either divide personally, so I cannot say from experience. But to have life stripped of both, to be alone in such a profound way, the very ones who stood for your past and your future taken away, must be devastating.

There is one intriguing detail of poignancy in the text: "with her was a large crowd from the town." It was not uncommon in this era for mourners to be hired. But unless this is an extremely unusual circumstance, a widow would not have the resources to hire mourners. Those who come do so of their own volition. For the sake of this woman, in remembrance of her son and acknowledging what faces her without child or partner, a large number of townspeople go with her. It reminds me of the tradition for funerals here in our small town. People who outlived friends and neighbors and even family will die—and the church will still be packed. It is just what community does.

Luke notes that what links Jesus to this unfolding scene is compassion. *Compassion* is an unusual word in Greek. Its root has to do with the intestines or the "guts," a part of the anatomy some ancient peoples associated with the seat of human emotion or passion. So when this story connects what Jesus sees with compassion for this widow, you can liken it to that feeling deep in the pit of your stomach when you see something—or someone—in dire need. That feeling that urges you to do something, whatever you can, to convey empathy, to transform the situation as you are able.

In this instance, the transformation is dramatic. Jesus touches the funeral bier and bids the young man to rise. Then, as if it were the most natural thing to do, the dead man does just that.

Luke does not offer any explanation. Transformation is not about mechanics or recording secret incantations and gestures that would suggest we could do the same if only we knew the right thing to say or do. Maybe that is why Luke simply mentions that touch and words were involved. Compassion always involves those two things, in one way or another. If we would express compassion in any meaningful way, if we would transform situations that resonate deep in our spirits: we need to be ready to touch what seems beyond reach. We need to be ready to speak what appears beyond hearing. Transformation is not about what we all knew would happen. Transformation is about opening ourselves and our world to outcomes and turnings that totally catch us off guard in their grace and wonder.

Look at this story. It is not simply that someone who stopped breathing resumes breathing. The young man is not just restored to life—he is restored to relationship. "Jesus gave him to his mother," Luke says in extraordinary understatement. For a bereft mother, for a lifeless son, transformation reverses the course and reopens their futures to one another.

But family reunion does not end this story. Transformation reaches now into the community of people who had walked with this widow in the solidarity of mourning. Had they not been there with her, had they not engaged in a touching act of compassion, they might have been surprised when they heard such news. But because they shared her pain and journey, they now share her joy. Grief and fear give way to glory and witness. They are no longer the same. They, like this widow, like her son, have been transformed.

It can be that way for us as well. Like this young man, we may experience restoration that brings us back to places of life from habits and values and pronouncements that had death written all over them. Like this widow, we may experience transformation when doors thought closed and relationships thought lost become open and found once more. And like this community, transformation may find and surprise us when we show compassion for others.

I pray, God, not only your favorable look but your transforming touch and word upon my life.

ENCOUNTERING JESUS TODAY

Name the persons who have looked with compassion on you. Ask yourself: *How did that person and that compassion change my life? How did they touch me? How did they speak to me?* Call to mind an individual in your community (church or wider) you believe is in need of compassion. Put yourself in her shoes. How would such compassion look to her: what would touch her and speak to her most deeply? Decide how you will act with such compassion on her behalf this week. Pray that God will use your compassion to transform her—and to transform you.

DAY FIVE

Canaanite Woman   *Matthew 15:21-28*

There she goes again, speaking up when she should just be still. Doesn't she know her place? Doesn't she know people like her don't belong here? For crying out loud, she's a . . .

According to Matthew, *she* is a Canaanite woman, a Gentile who has no place among the people of Israel. Matthew indicates this story occurs in or near the "district of Tyre and Sidon." These were Gentile territories. The story puts Jesus and the disciples— and with them, the church—right in the middle of outsiders and outlaws, in the sense of those who live outside the law of Torah. And if you risk venturing outside the safety zone of sanctuary, whether sanctuary goes defined by a white-frame building or a familiar neighborhood or a long-standing tradition about how or with whom we do things around here, the world is apt to make its presence known.

That presence in Matthew's story comes in the form of a woman who cries out for mercy on behalf of her daughter. The response to her cries by both Jesus and disciples underwhelm. At first, Jesus does not answer her. The disciples, as in other encounters with interrupting children or hungering crowds, urge Jesus to send her away. To which Jesus only says, "I was sent only to the lost sheep of the house of Israel." No one bothers to address her. It is as if she were not there.

What does that feel like? Occasionally we hear terrible stories of individuals assaulted on a city street, in full view of residents and passersby. The victim cries out for help, only to be ignored; only to be treated as if he or she does not exist. We need not venture into those extreme situations, though, to know what this Canaanite woman experiences. Sometimes, we like to think that uncomfortable persons—and issues—will leave us alone if we ignore them long enough. And sometimes they do. But at other times, they persist. Like this woman, they keep crying out loud when we'd rather have them pass quietly out of our presence.

Remarkably, Jesus makes a 180-degree turn. From pronouncing the inappropriateness of giving the children's food to dogs his words change to praise of her trust. Commending her faith, Jesus concludes "let it be done for you as you wish." Her daughter, a Gentile, is healed by Jesus, who had just said he was sent only to the lost sheep of Israel. There the story ends.

Or is it there the story begins?

Keep in mind that the theme for this chapter is transformation. One might judge the previous story about raising the widow's son the pinnacle of transformative encounters. After all, what can top the transformation of life restored from death? I would humbly suggest the transformation of Jesus by this woman. Jesus is not the same after the encounter—at the very least, his words are not the same before and after.

Some may consider the idea that Jesus was subject to change to be scandalous or irreverent. I find it redemptive and hopeful. If God as revealed in Christ is not open to change, why do we pray for God's intercession, seeking transformation in a particular situation? Why is Jonah sent to Nineveh, and what does it mean to read, "God *changed his mind* about the calamity that he had said he would bring upon them; and he did not do it" (Jonah 3:10, emphasis added)?

Even more pertinent to our reflection during Lent: if God as revealed in Christ is not open to transformation, what happened when Jesus died? Was it all mere appearance, as the ancient Docetists argued, since in their view spirit could never die and Jesus was wholly spirit? Or was the death of Jesus, in a way that acknowledges mystery at the heart of theology, a transformative experience in the very heart of God, for which the Resurrection was the defiant and redemptive reply?

It is possible to push the theme of God in Christ's transformation too far. We are not the architects of God's nature. On the other hand, theology has at times pushed the theme of God's immutable nature far beyond what the Hebrew and Christian stories affirm. It is not God's unchangeable nature that results in the choice of a rainbow after the choice of a flood. It is not God's unchangeable nature revealed in Jesus' birth in a manger and Jesus' death on a cross. God consistently opens up to being affected by the creation God loves. The Incarnation reveals the radical degree of change undertaken for the sake of the beloved.

Jesus took the disciples into the Gentile region of Tyre and Sidon, and there they encountered a Canaanite woman who would not stop crying out loud until she was heard. It is *always* that way for the church. Jesus leads us to places, and persons, outside the confines and control of our sanctuaries and our traditions. Jesus leads us not only in mission, where transformation comes in what we can do for and with others. Jesus leads us for the sake of our transformation *through* those others.

Christ of the opened heart, open me to change for the sake of another's good, and for the sake of your good in me.

Encountering Jesus Today

Jesus initially speaks a harsh word in response to the Canaanite woman's request. But his words change, and help is given. Consider some one, some group, whom you do not hold in high esteem. Read this story as if it were directed to your relationship with that other. What change might this narrative evoke on your part: in your opinion about them, in your action on behalf of them? Take a step in that direction today. Follow the leading of Jesus in prayer and example. Be open to transformation by God through that other, in the light of Jesus' encounter with this woman.

Week Five

EMPOWERED

JOHN DONNE'S OBSERVATION that "no man is an island" speaks to more than the intricate ways our lives connect to one another. With the right conditions, our lives can be empowered by others. We may find in the presence or example of another—a teacher, a companion, a friend, sometimes even a critic—the ability to live in a way we had not thought possible or dared before. This chapter considers people whose encounters with Jesus bring empowerment. A woman whose illness prevented her from exercising hospitality finds the ability to resume that role when Jesus heals her. A man whom Jesus freed from a hopeless past finds the wherewithal to accept a challenging call. One group, nurtured by Jesus' ministry, becomes a source of ministry for Jesus' community. An outcast discovers in Jesus' welcome of him the power to offer both welcome and justice. Two travelers discover in a stranger's words and breaking of bread the ability to serve as Easter's witnesses.

Transformative encounter, explored in the previous chapter, does not bring change purely for the sake of change. Such encounter potentially gives us the means to act as disciples in callings both familiar and new. Empowerment for discipleship is crucial and it is risky. The Lenten journey, reflecting our own sojourn in life, reveals other forces at work in this world. Such powers seek to silence truth, to deny justice, and to withhold compassion. Lives gospeled by encounter with Jesus find empowerment to counter those forces through ministry exercised for the sake of others in Christ's own example.

DAY ONE

Before Alzheimer's descended upon her, my mother was a gracious host. My childhood memories are filled with a succession of family gatherings around the dining room table. As I look back, preparing the meals and getting the house ready must have been a chore for her. But if it was, she did not show that discomfort at table. Mom seemed to truly enjoy a full house, when the leaves on the dining room table had to be extended and card tables set up to provide a place for all. And it would not take any coaxing that I recall for Mom to sit at the piano after dinner and play, whether we all sat and listened or joined in singing Mitch Miller songs (now I *am* dating myself!). Years after her death, I still think what a gift it would have been if, for one day, the dementia might have lifted and she could have taken her place once more at table and piano.

We don't always find our place restored to what it had been. Such circumstances grieve us. But sometimes, and through someone, restoration does come. Those experiences offer hope and encouragement—and a calling to go and do likewise for others as we are able.

Consider the story from Mark. Its core is brief. Jesus enters a home and heals a woman, who then serves a meal. Some at this point spin off into conjectures raised by Mark's identifying this woman as Simon's mother-in-law. What, then, of Simon's wife or children? What happens to them when Simon abandons vocation (and therefore livelihood) and follows this Jesus? These are intriguing questions. The problem is, they are absolutely ignored by the Gospels in general, and Mark 1 in particular. The focus remains tight on this encounter with Jesus that brings healing to Simon's mother-in-law. But not healing alone. The other intriguing aspect of this story is that it does not end with the action of Jesus but with the action of the woman.

"She began to *serve* them." *Serve* is a loaded word in the New Testament. Its root word in Greek, *diakoneo*, originated with serving tables. Your church may even have a committee whose name derives from this word: deacons, diaconate. In the New Testament, when this word is used in reference to the church or especially to men, it tends to be translated as "minister." So we could just as accurately say: Simon's mother-in-law *ministered* to them.

Is it demeaning for Mark to suggest the outcome of her restorative encounter with Jesus to be waiting on tables? Remember the context of these times. The most important obligation of a host to guests was hospitality. It was not mere courtesy but a vital tradition. In her illness, this woman would have been prevented from fulfilling her status as elder woman of the household. The healing empowers her to practice hospitality, to be the gracious host. The fact that the New Testament ends up appropriating this word as the language of ministry ought not to be dismissed as coincidence. Ministry and welcome define one another, then and now.

So thanks to her empowering encounter with Jesus, she who was healed now ministers. Perhaps you hear in her story the whispers—or shouts—of personal experiences, in which empowerment came through restoration of place. It may have come in the restoration of health, following a debilitating condition that had restricted you from valued work or cherished relationships. Can you remember your gratitude for the personnel and caregivers who brought you back to health? It may have come through the encouragement of a companion or friend to resume a part of your life that had been interrupted or to take on something never attempted. Again, can you recall your thankfulness to those others for being able to step back into that role or assume it for the first time? Those who make it possible for us to return to or to find our place empower us as Christ did this woman.

Empowerment that restores place may take surprising turns. I remember an afternoon with my mother at the Alzheimer's care unit where she resided. The conversation had been rambling, and it would not be long before even her rambling disappeared under the fog of dementia. But that afternoon, a warm spring day as I recall, we adjourned to a porch swing. As we rocked, she quickly fell asleep. I thought about how the one who rocked me to sleep now passed into a quiet and, for the moment, peaceful rest. Our reversal of roles became clear—as did a powerful sense of gratitude for all she had done for me, much of the time when I could do little or nothing for myself. I wish I could say empowerment and restoration came to her. I cannot.

But I can say that afternoon on the swing became a time and memory I continually came back to during her illness and dying. Our time together that day empowered me for the days yet to come. In a way I find difficult to express or explain, save to claim it as my experience: on that swing, she who was *not* healed or restored ministered to me. Such is the power of love.

Lift me up, O Christ, that I may be in a position to uplift others. In your name.

Encountering Jesus Today

What has your faith empowered you to do? For the moment, don't consider your participation in faith community. Consider your roles in family, in the wider community. How does your service in those settings grow out of your encounter with Christ? How, and from whom, have you experienced restoration in those places? How, and to whom, might you be the one who could bring empowerment and mediate Christ's presence where restoration is needed?

Day Two

Gerasene Demoniac   Mark 5:1-20

Our son works with incarcerated juvenile offenders. He began his career several years ago as a counselor and recently was promoted to a coordinator position for the facility. The new job possessed ample challenges. Within a month of his assuming it, however, the sex offender coordinator for the facility took a job elsewhere. It was determined that, until a new hire had been made, our son would handle that position as well. The differences between work with the general population of juvenile offenders and sex offenders are enormous. Previously he had not worked in the units set apart for housing and treating sex offenders. It was a population he had chosen not to work with—but now he had no choice. The next several months proved taxing, not only because he was tasked with doing two full-time jobs in the space of one. Looking back, he speaks of having learned and grown from working in a field he would not have chosen. And to put a touch of parental pride on this story, the folks among and for whom he has worked have benefited as well.

Sometimes, growth and empowerment come from encounters whose outcomes we would not have chosen. The story of the Gerasene demoniac is one of the lengthier narratives in the Gospel of Mark. Its nuances and anachronisms could fill an entire chapter if not a book all on its own. But for now, we will skip the cemetery and the dialogue with Legion and the rush of pigs off a cliff—and go straight to the *really* intriguing part of the story: Jesus' refusal to allow the man, now clothed and in his right mind, to follow him.

On first reading, Jesus' action might seem extremely odd if not cruel. The individual is begging Jesus to let him come along. Just a moment before, the crowd saw the fellow looking sane instead of the raving lunatic they were all used to, and they begged Jesus to leave. Jesus responded by heading for the boat. So why shouldn't this man, whose transformation rendered his community not joyful but fearful, want to get into the boat and head out with the one who changed his life? *Can't you get me out of here, Jesus—I mean, look at these people!*

Jesus refused.

Whether the refusal caught the healed man by surprise or not, it probably does us. We may have some empathy with being in places and with people we want no part of. In my opinion much of the current obsession with the "rapture" springs from the desire to extract oneself from folks and situations we would rather not face. Jesus, however, was not into the faith-as-escape-pod mentality. "Go home to your friends, and tell them how much the Lord has done for you, and what mercy he has shown you."

Sometimes we view Jonah as having it tough—told to go to those hated Ninevite strangers. But sometimes, the far harder journey is back home, back to our relationships, back to the places where everybody knows just who and how we are—and to speak, and live, in a new way. That is just what Jesus dispatches this individual to do. To bring not just a new word to the old gang, but in his changed self to embody that new word, so that he becomes the lived synonym of mercy.

Jesus' refusal to let the fellow tag along in the boat empowers this man's life and witness in this community. Did Jesus' action cause a powerful revival to sweep through the cities of the Decapolis? Did Jesus' action even reassure the individual that going home was the only good choice? We don't know. Mark only tells us that the man does just as Jesus says and that everyone is "amazed." Remember, though, that amazement in the Gospels does not equate with belief. It may be a precursor to faith, or it may be a false spring.

We do not know how this story plays out in these communities. Perhaps they do receive the message brought in word and in person by the man now healed. Or perhaps they settle back into unchanged routines and presumptions, considering his new state of mind yet another odd development in his odd life. The lack of a packaged ending reminds us we have to furnish the outcomes in our times, as they did in theirs, to the intrusion of grace and the facing of fear in our lives.

Second Corinthians 1:20 speaks of Christ as being a yes to all of God's promises. Mark 5 tempers that with the truth that encounter with Jesus may bring a no to some of our seekings. Even the most understandable requests, such as this man's plea to go along with Jesus, may find a no. We do not always get to choose what comes to us in life or how and where God empowers us to serve. Sometimes the path lies in those ways and among those people unconsidered, whether because we hardly know them . . . or because we know them all too well.

God, whose wisdom routinely escapes our own, may I hear in the no to what I seek, the yes to what you would make possible.

Encountering Jesus Today

Recall times when you have sought to "steal away with Jesus," only to find a no to that request. Where did you end up and, looking back, why? How did you find empowerment to face that unchosen situation? Consider your spiritual journey at this moment and any circumstances that would incline you to seek escape in faith. What would you be avoiding? What would you be missing? Imagine Jesus saying to you now: *Go home to* _____. Fill in the blank for yourself. Consider how that "going home" might lead you in ways you would not have chosen.

Day Three

I loved my home church. It nurtured my faith. It provided a host of activities for children and youth and adults, offering spiritual growth, recreation, and fellowship for every age. Its music program excelled and instilled a joy and appreciation for Spirit's movement through notes and chords as much as verse and text. I loved that community. But love cannot always overlook the faults of the beloved as if they do not matter.

My home church was built in great measure by the efforts of women. To be sure, unlike many congregations today and even then, we had a large and active men's group in the church. It was not unusual to have almost a hundred men turn out for the monthly meetings of the "Brotherhood." Their fall *Wurstmarts* and Lenten fish fries drew huge crowds. They did good work. But their efforts were matched, if not exceeded, by the Women's Fellowship groups. Their service within the congregation and in the wider community was striking. Women formed the great majority of our Sunday school teachers—and with a program involving three hundred or more children, that involved a lot of teachers.

Women worked and ministered everywhere in that church—except two places. One place was the Church Council. When I entered seminary in 1972, the Council was still a men-only club. The second place was the pulpit and the lectern. When I was in college, I often served as a liturgist. One Sunday, when I had a stomach full of butterflies, I asked Faye if she could do at least the opening readings until I felt better. Faye was one of my all-time favorites there: besides teaching the adult Sunday school class, she was a high school teacher and a very competent and devout woman whom I was graced to have as a friend. It was a difficult decision for her, precisely because women did not do that kind of thing there. But she did.

Why spend so much time talking about the ways things used to be in a now-defunct Evangelical and Reformed UCC church in northwest St. Louis?

As much as things change, some things regrettably stay the same. At times, we in the church engage in finger pointing at first-century Judaism for restrictive attitudes toward women that Jesus overcomes. There is debate these days as to how much those attitudes reflected the situation "on the ground" back then and how much they were stereotypes the church used in its later conflict with Judaism. What is clear and beyond debate is Jesus' openness to the presence and participation of women in the community he gathered.

Our awareness of the women in Jesus' community comes largely through the Crucifixion and Resurrection narratives. But Luke 8 offers a glimpse into the presence and participation of women in Jesus' ministry and the community's life well before those final days. Luke singles out Mary Magdalene, who has garnered much attention of late—and rightly so. He also names Joanna, the wife of a royal official, and Susanna. And then Luke adds, "and many others." "Many others" suggests that the presence of women among the followers of Jesus is not an isolated or trivial matter. While not specifying the nature of their encounters (except for Mary Magdalene), Luke first affirms the *empowerment* those encounters generated. Speaking of Mary and Joanna and Susanna and the many others, Luke says they "provided for them [Jesus and the disciples] out of their resources."

To say the women use their own resources might be surprising, since a common stereotype about women of that period is that they would have had no resources other than their husband's. The text suggests these are women of means, and that out of encounter with Jesus they choose to employ those means in the service of community. Secondly, and perhaps even more telling, is this word *provide*. We have already looked at this word in some detail in the first reading of this chapter: *diakoneo*. This is the word often translated in other passages as "minister." These are not just women of means, as liberating as that may be. These are women of *ministry*.

Jesus had no problem with the ministry of women. It was encounter with Jesus that empowered their ministry. The irony, and a cruel one at that, is that the community of Jesus has not always and everywhere honored the practices of the One we say we follow. To be sure, we are happy to have the support generated by women's labor in fund-raising, teaching our children, and serving in "appropriate" ways in outreach. But too often, like my beloved home church, we fail to empower in ministry those whom Christ has already empowered for ministry. They, and we, suffer for it.

Mary Magdalene and Joanna and Susanna and many others: what names and groups take their overlooked places among us? That is, who are the ones whose lives and ministries or their very presence find empowerment by Jesus, and even provide for the community of Jesus, only to be left waiting to see if the church will ever embrace those ministries?

God of boundless grace and providence, help me to provide for the good of your community by supporting all through whom you minister.

ENCOUNTERING JESUS TODAY

Who are the ones whose presence and ministry in your community goes neglected or unrecognized? Hold that individual or group in prayer. Commit to taking some personal action that will convey support and recognition of them and of their ministry.

Day Four

Zacchaeus *Luke 19:1-10*

Sometimes I think little children get all the good Bible stories! Think about the narratives we tend to teach to the youngest among us: the Garden of Eden, an ark full of animals with a rainbow at the end, a shepherd boy who became king—and a "wee little man" named Zacchaeus. Indeed, some adults might know this story mainly through the primary-age song it inspired:

> *Zacchaeus was a wee little man, and a wee little man was he.*
> *He climbed up in a sycamore tree, for the Lord he wanted to see.*

And then there's the part in the song where all the parents and grandparents get a good chuckle when they see their children, imitating Jesus by imitating grown-ups, shake their fingers up in the air and shout, "Zacchaeus, you come down!"

It is a cute song. But as with other Bible stories we tell to the young ones, it goes much deeper than cuteness. Zacchaeus may have been a wee little man, but he was also a rich little weasel as well. And most likely, a ruthless one to boot. Wee little Zacchaeus was a chief tax collector, an agent of the Roman occupation government in the district around Jericho. Such officials would pay the Roman governor the equivalent of a franchise fee, authorizing them to collect various taxes in a given region. Profits were made in direct proportion to how effectively and often pitilessly the taxes were collected. Zacchaeus shares much in common with Levi, whose encounter with Jesus we explored in the first chapter. Both were outcasts and pariahs.

Such a man was Zacchaeus, wee and little not only in physical stature but communal standing. Zacchaeus embodied all that was wrong with life in an occupied country. He was an incarnation of greed, an example of what would become of you if you turned your back on your traditions and your people. Imagine then the deafening silence when the itinerant rabbi calls out to the person whose very name may have been that town's synonym for a four-letter word not to be used in mixed company: "Zacchaeus, hurry and come down; for I must stay at your house today." It is not long before keepers of the community standards start pronouncing self-righteous judgment. Tongues wag about a rabbi who goes as guest into a sinner's house. For them, the encounter comes to a screeching halt.

But for Zacchaeus, the gospel encounter has only begun.

Almost in defense of his self-invited guest's openness, Zacchaeus makes an announcement that reveals conventional wisdom about him might need to be revised. He offers to split his bankroll with the poor—and, out of his remaining half, to restore anything defrauded fourfold.

Zacchaeus's act can be viewed in two ways. On the one hand, people could hear his offer to give half of everything to the poor (some of whom he probably helped to impoverish) and restore fourfold anything defrauded mainly as confirmation that this fellow really did have a truckload of Jericho's hard-earned money. The other view of Zacchaeus's act, however, is to accept the generosity for what it is. What he offers is not in character with the man Zacchaeus has been up to this point. Has he arrived at sainthood yet? Probably not. The text doesn't say he turned in his resignation as tax collector. Yet something has happened.

In the estimation of Jesus, what has happened is salvation: "Salvation has come to this house." Has salvation come in Jesus' presence or in Zacchaeus's act? The answer is yes. Encounter with Jesus' hospitality toward him empowers Zacchaeus's gracious and just response toward all. Salvation comes when divine grace and human response welcome each other.

So it is with us. Salvation comes when we realize God does not need us to decide who is and who is not worthy of grace. The

Cross rendered that decision quite well, thank you. God's welcome of us in Christ invites our lives to be shaped by such grace. The shaping begins within, in our spirits, but by no means does that tell the whole tale. The goal of our empowerment by encounter with Jesus is not simply hearts strangely warmed. Christ *empowers* us to live as he lived toward others: affording grace, seeking justice, enacting love.

With Zacchaeus, may we allow God the freedom to empower us, that we might move beyond the presumptions of our past in order to be gracious and just to whomever God chooses. Even to this wee little man named Zacchaeus. Even to his much-maligned, scandalous-to-our-ears kin today. Even, if the truth be told, to the grumblers of Jericho . . . and the likes of you and me.

Bring your salvation to me, O God, that you might bring your salvation through me.

ENCOUNTERING JESUS TODAY

Read the following verse excerpt aloud, putting your name in the blank, imagining Christ speaking them to you: "_____, I must stay at your house today." What preparations would you make in response to this declaration: in the interior of your life? in your relationships? What would you set aside? What would you take on or practice in a new way? List these things. Pick out one priority for your inner life and one for your relationship with others. Write down these two priorities and place the piece of paper where you will see it at the beginning and end of each day. Prayerfully commit to seeking such change in your life in these two areas and reflecting on them each day.

DAY FIVE

Emmaus Road Disciples   *Luke 24:13-35*

There is great uncertainty about the exact location of the "Emmaus" referred to in this story. Most ancient manuscripts relate the distance between Emmaus and Jerusalem as sixty *stadia* (about seven miles), though some manuscripts indicate 160 *stadia*. The latter figure agrees with one town called Emmaus. The shorter distance has two contenders for Luke's "Emmaus."

The fact that we do not know exactly which Emmaus destination these two distraught followers had in mind reflects the nature of the journey they took. For while Luke notes they were going to Emmaus, that seems to be about the only sure thing in their lives at the moment. Too much had happened, and now they were out walking, dazed, trying to make sense of it all.

I dare say we all have traveled similar roads, and we may be on one now. We may walk, we may drive, we may immerse ourselves in wilderness or burrow in to the creature comforts of home. But in any case, when we find ourselves trying to sort through certainties turned upside down or hopes suddenly dashed or experiences difficult to process, much less understand, it really doesn't matter what the signposts say or the GPS receiver indicates for our coordinates. When we are on that journey, we are on the road to Emmaus.

It is a road best traveled in company with others. This is not to dismiss the need for solitude. Times and places apart have their role, and a critical one, in discerning the way ahead when all the doors seem to be in the wrong places and all the old answers don't seem to work. But we have been formed of God for something more than solitary existence. We have been formed for relationship with God. We have been formed for community with others. And when one or the other stands threatened or seems impossible, we do well to seek the aid of a companion.

So at the very outset of Luke's story, there is hope in these two choosing to travel together. Presented with the deadly reality of Good Friday and the seeming in-credibility of Easter morning, they choose to face this crisis of faith in community. Their choice to journey together may in fact open them to the possibility of presence suggested in Jesus' promise: "where two or three are gathered in my name, I am there among them" (Matt. 18:20). The promise does not require the gathered people to have all the answers ahead of time. Jesus comes, not just when we're full of praise choruses as we sit in our places with bright shiny faces. Jesus comes when the gathering laments and questions. Jesus comes, not just into sanctuaries chock full of symbols and signs but on journeys where we may not even be sure where we are headed. Jesus comes on the road to Emmaus to these disciples—and on that road to us—for the purpose of empowerment.

In the case of these disciples, empowerment begins with interpreting words known for a long time but broken open in new ways. Even when we think we have all the answers (or questions), we don't. Just ask Job. Job too had questions and wonderings. But God did not withhold speaking from the whirlwind until Job had everything right and in order. God met Job where he was, as God meets these disciples where they are, and as God seeks to meet us where we are, physically and spiritually. That is the Emmaus truth.

But truth is not apprehended in word alone. In retrospect, hearts may have burned while scripture was broken open. But truth was not recognized until bread was broken. Faith is not solely a matter of the disposition of minds or even hearts. Faith is not merely propositional or emotional. Faith, Christian faith, faith as broken open to us in Christ, is incarnational. It is sacramental. It comes mediated in the texture of bread and the taste of wine, the splash of water, and the shouted silence of an emptied tomb. Such things open eyes and evoke recognition.

When Emmaus road recognition finally does come, Jesus vanishes. To the cynical, nothing has changed for those two disciples—or for us. It is still just them, just us, on this way.

But something has happened, for which the departure of Jesus represents yet another step in empowerment. The ones who had been followers now move forward and outward to become apostles. Their witness is empowered by the experience of the risen Christ even as it is necessitated by his departure. For with Jesus gone, who will tell the story of recognition but those two?

So it is with us. Our recognition of the God who comes to us in Christ is not a secret password that gives us entry into an exclusive club. Our recognition of God in Christ empowers and sends us as witnesses to the One who meets us on our Emmaus "roads."

May we be graced by the One who comes to us not only in broken bread but also in the brokenness of life, to empower us for holy journey and faithful witness.

Christ of Emmaus and all our journeys, open our eyes to see you, and strengthen our faith to follow you all along the way.

Encountering Jesus Today

Consider individuals whose faith you respect and whom you trust. Which one of them would you want to join you on your Emmaus road—that is, the road where you would feel free to talk about the deep concerns and questions of your faith? If you feel comfortable doing so, approach that person about being such a partner in exploring one another's faith and being open to the presence of Christ. If you do not feel comfortable doing this, pray for what might make it possible for you to do so—or to find someone you could trust in this journey.

OPEN-ENDED

PARENTS, SPONSORS, AND CONGREGATION witness the pastor pour water from a baptismal bowl onto the head of a little child. In the best of such moments, eyes moisten, heads nod, and memories flash. But not memories alone. Some may wonder: what comes next? How will she grow into, or away from, Christian community like so many others before her? Baptism is not vaccination, insuring a predefined outcome. Baptism is a door opening and choices beginning.

The faith journey has always been like that. We might have preferred the Gospels to have tidied up their stories of encounter with Jesus into self-contained packages with guaranteed outcomes and no loose ends. But neither faith nor life proceeds that way, nor do the narratives of encounter considered in this final chapter. Ten are healed, while one returns to give thanks. What of the other nine? A host is upbraided for a lack of hospitality that insinuates a paucity of love. Does he learn and then practice that table's lesson? Some who would follow Jesus once they finish pressing business are told no business is more pressing. Do they follow? A scribe is told he is not far from the kingdom of God. Is "not far" close enough? Jesus astounds crowds. Do they remain content with astonishment or seek something more?

The gospeling of these lives by encounter with Jesus produces open-ended rather than conclusive finales. Their stories invite us to wonder not only what becomes of these people but what becomes of us when we stand where they did. For like baptism, encounter with Jesus always has been and always will be a door opening and choices beginning.

Ten Lepers   *Luke 17:11-19*

Do what you're told, and you won't get in trouble. How many times have you heard that before? How many times have you *said* that before? *Do what you're told* is a dynamic that can come to the fore in family life between parents and children. It sometimes arises when lengthy protests of "why" lead to impasse; the time for dialogue is over, and the time for action has arrived.

Do what you're told is also a dynamic that permeates some forms of religious observance. Deuteronomy 28 concludes its lengthy recital of covenant law by spelling out blessings for keeping said law and curses for disobedience. Christian tradition has sometimes attempted to paint all of Judaism with the broad brush of legalism, conveniently forgetting that the church both ancient and modern has often proclaimed its own version of *do what you're told and you won't get in trouble* as gospel. On the right, we translate this gospel into personal moral strictures that aim to clone preferred lifestyles. On the left, we translate this gospel into self-declared progressive policies that reflect our version of enlightened politics. All sides weigh in with admonishing tones that fall somewhere between a prophet and a second-grade teacher: *do what you're told (by us) and you won't get in trouble.*

Unfortunately, the outcome presumed in that admonishment is just not true to life.

A clear case in point is the story of the ten lepers. For now, set aside all the Thanksgiving or stewardship sermons you may have heard preached on this text, in which the focus centers on the one leper who returns to give thanks to Jesus. As important as that man's action may be, let us rather direct our attention to the other nine. And let us do so with the clear understanding that they end up in trouble for doing *exactly* what Torah and Jesus tell them to do.

"Go and show yourselves to the priests."

It may be unsettling to think that doing what Jesus tells us could get us into trouble. But this story is by no means alone in the Gospels in suggesting that very truth. Jesus gets into a boat with the disciples and tells them to shove off—and *then* they encounter the storm. Isn't Jesus supposed to get us out of storms, instead of putting us there in the first place? Then again, words about taking up crosses and being innocent as doves yet wise as serpents indicate that encounter with Jesus will sometimes lead us into troublesome spots.

Back to this story: the ten lepers all do exactly what Jesus tells them to do. They set into motion the ritual for having themselves declared clean by the priests. While healing had taken place, leprosy entailed social as well as physical consequences. Only a priestly declaration could restore these ten to community. But then one leper breaks ranks and turns around to express thanks to God and Jesus. In strictly legal terms, this one—not the nine—ignores the rules. This one goes outside the boundaries of requirements by initiating a spontaneous and unsolicited return of thanks. Luke, ever the champion of outsiders, may have found it hard to suppress a smile as he goes on to write that this one returnee was, of all things, a Samaritan.

"But the other nine," Jesus asks, "where are they?"

The awkward silence on this point in the text is understandable: they are exactly where Jesus sent them, doing just what Jesus told them to do. Too often the church interprets this story as condemning these nine. It does not have to be. Rather, this story of the nine can be about the open-ended nature of encounter with Jesus, then and now. The truth is, we do not know what became of the nine. We do not know what happened after they left the priests. Did they resume life and relationship with gratitude for healing, or did they retain bitterness over all those years of suffering? Did they quickly forget the One who brought healing, or did they return

later seeking Jesus, only to find he had already moved on? Did they
_____ ? (You fill in the blank.)

The point of asking such questions is not to determine the fate of these nine men. The point is: what about us? Does encounter with Jesus for us boil down to doing what we are told—by law, by church, by pastor—in order to avoid trouble? If we can fault the action by the nine in this text at all, it lies in this matter. Following the letter of the law, even when it comes to the words of Jesus, does not guarantee faithful response to the gospel's intention. Grace bids us sometimes to break routines and rules for spontaneous and unsolicited responses that aim not to avoid trouble but to embrace and express joy.

We can easily neglect holy encounter when the accretion of rules and policies stand where relationship ought to be. Or, holy encounter may prompt an urge to turn, to give thanks, to render service to the One who graces us on the way. Where the other nine are is a question past its time. The question whose time has come is: where are we?

May we do as we are shown, O God, by the enacted mercy of Christ.

Encountering Jesus Today

Recall a time in your life when faith was mostly a matter of doing what you were told. What did you learn from those experiences about yourself, about God, about discipleship? Read aloud Luke 17:17. Write a narrative in response to Jesus' question "Where are they?" about those nine; tell it from the perspective and experience of your own life.

DAY TWO

One way of deepening our understanding of a biblical story is to enter it from the perspective of a character in the narrative. For example, put yourself in the place of Simon the Pharisee in this story. What do you see and hear taking place in that scene? How does this story "feel" from the perspective of Simon? We have already explored a slightly differing narrative of Simon's encounter in this book's prologue. Then we looked at the encounter from the perspective and in remembrance of the woman's action. Now we consider this encounter from the perspective of the action—or, more accurately, inaction—of the host, a Pharisee named Simon.

Those who like to portray Jesus' role in first-century Judaism as a theological wrecking ball face a problem in this story. A Pharisee, one of those we so frequently depict as gospel opponents, has invited Jesus to break bread at his table. And Jesus goes. Jesus' table fellowship, often celebrated as his radical connection to sinners and tax collectors, apparently remains open to those on the respectable side of the tracks as well. Given the other options for affiliation in first-century Judaism—Sadducee, Pharisee, Zealot, Essene, Herodian—Jesus' ministry and teachings arguably come closest in spirit to those of the Pharisees. So we should not view the setting of this encounter as "enemy territory" for Jesus. It is home ground, every bit as much as dining in the house of Zacchaeus or worshiping in the synagogue at Nazareth. But home ground does not mean all is well. Encounter slips into challenge not because of Simon's identity as a Pharisee but because of his behavior as a host.

It is not only Simon's treatment of Jesus or lack thereof that prompts the accusative parable of the debtors. Underlying this entire exchange between the two is Simon's "reception" of the woman who so scandalously anoints and even kisses the feet of

Jesus. Simon's thoughts (inexplicably revealed to Luke) dwell on the ineptitude of a prophet who can't recognize what sort of woman this is. It is as if Simon would rather not even acknowledge her, much less welcome her.

Simon does pay attention when Jesus addresses him with a parable. Simon even grasps the meaning of Jesus' words on love and forgiveness. "You have judged rightly," Jesus affirms. But understanding words and putting them into practice are two different things. When Jesus transitions from anonymous parable into personal accusation, Simon is left speechless. Literally. We hear nothing of or from Simon again.

So what happens to Simon the Pharisee?

As suggested at the outset of this reading, put yourself in Simon's shoes. A guest in your home not only upbraids you for poor hospitality but also infers that such lack of attention betrays a far deeper flaw on your part: the absence of love. How do you respond? Thank the guest for that piece of insight? Anoint the guest's lap with the soup intended for the first course? Show him the door? Or do you wonder, *What if the guest is right? Where have I gone wrong?*

Encounter with Jesus does not always tell us what we want to hear about ourselves or the world around us. Grace is not the equivalent of "anything goes." Grace provides the acceptance to see ourselves as God sees us and to live into the new life God seeks for us.

Grace underlies this encounter: the grace of this woman toward Jesus, the grace of Jesus in recognizing her act as one of love—and yes, the grace of Jesus toward Simon. If Jesus had no hope or love for Simon—or Pharisees in general—why bother showing up for dinner with someone judged beyond redemption? Why bother offering the parable? Why bother affirming Simon "judges rightly" but leaves something to be desired on the follow-through? But Jesus does bother. Jesus does not tailor the gospel to make it more palatable. Jesus proclaims and embodies the gospel to make it more pertinent to those places in our hearts and lives caught in the same struggle between judging rightly and *doing* the right. Jesus does so for Simon and for us.

The narrative leaves the ending unresolved. We do not know what happens to Simon after this tabled encounter. Then again, what happens when the gospel confronts us on matters we might prefer to ignore or deny in our lives? What happens when it confronts self-righteousness that discounts our culpability of sin in comparison with the flagrant sin of those "other" people? What happens when Jesus says to us, through Simon, "the one to whom little is forgiven, loves little"?

Placing ourselves in Simon's shoes may be very discomforting. Yet, it may be the very place where the gospel's transformation of our lives comes to light—and to life.

May I receive and welcome you, Lord Jesus, even when grace means speaking the truth in love.

Encountering Jesus Today

Reflect on one aspect of faith that you find troublesome to practice. Identify reasons for that difficulty. As you do, consider how those reasons relate to what this practice of faith calls you to take on or give up—or perhaps even who it brings into your life. Imagine yourself at table with Jesus, discussing this matter. What words of encouragement, and challenge, might you hear?

Day Three

Would-Be Followers   *Luke 9:57-62*

Over the past two years, the Reverend Dr. Mark Miller has served as the Transitional Interim Conference Minister of the Pacific Northwest Conference of the United Church of Christ (my home conference). Mark makes light of the acronym for his title (TICM), saying he hopes his work does not lead too many people to hear it with an "off" at the end (as in, "tic 'em off"). His other trademark wordplay when he speaks to churches and church leaders explores variations on the theme: *Your windshield needs to be larger than your rearview mirror.* The image is not only striking—it is gospel.

Not one but three encounters comprise Luke 9:57-62. It is not coincidental that Luke places these three immediately after a passage where he reports not once but twice that Jesus "set his face to go to Jerusalem." From Luke 9:51 onward, the windshield is all about Jerusalem. The Gospel moves relentlessly from this point forward toward that destination. Here, as Jesus and disciples set out on that way, three individuals are encountered. The first and third offer to follow Jesus, while the second is invited by Jesus to follow him. But do they follow? Jesus replies to the first person's offer to follow "wherever you go" that "wherever" may mean having no place to call home. The second one responds to Jesus' invitation with a request to first bury his father, only to hear stern words about the dead burying the dead. The third one prefaces his offer to follow with a request to first say his good-byes at home. Jesus says to him—and actually to all three—that "no one who puts a hand to the plow and looks back is fit for the kingdom of God."

With that, the narrative comes to a close. With that, we hear nothing more of these three would-be followers.

We're tempted to presume, as with the rich young man, that these three walked away and did not follow. End of story. That certainly seems to be the position of the *New International Study Bible* of the NRSV, which subtitles this passage: "The Failure of Three Would-Be Followers." But did they fail? Whether they prove "fit" or not, according to Jesus' closing words, we do not know because Luke does not tell us. Since we do not know, the open-ended nature of their encounters invites us to consider our own fitness for God's sovereign realm.

That word *fit* is a critical one in Jesus' words. To be "unfit" sounds rather final, especially when it is linked to suitability for God's realm. But keep in mind that the Greek word translated as "fit" literally means "well placed." In other words, preparing to plow a field that lies ahead when your eyes are set in exactly the opposite direction is not a "well placed" posture to take. It doesn't mean you are inherently unfit to engage in plowing. It just means that being torn in two directions is not conducive to moving forward. Or, to use the admonition of my pastor and colleague: *your windshield needs to be larger than your rearview mirror.*

I have never plowed a field, so I cannot speak from direct knowledge about the fitness of hands on a plow and eyes staring backward. But I have driven a car. And I have learned, from tires drifting onto the rumble strips on the shoulder or across the center lane, that where you look tends to be where you steer. It's bad enough to be distracted by something off to the right or left but to drive forward with your eyes glued on the rearview mirror? No thanks.

At least, I say that now, and so I think would you. But do we follow that advice in our lives? And do we follow that advice in our churches? Good religious folk and good religious institutions can be notorious for oversized rearview mirrors and undersized windshields. "That's not how we do things around here" are the bywords, though not the only words, of that truth among us. When we pay more attention to precedent than possibility, when we confuse learning from history with reproducing bygone days (and sometimes days that never were, except in nostalgia's imagination): we are not "well placed" for the movement inherent in God's sovereign realm. We are just positioning ourselves for more of the same.

Luke never does get around to telling us what becomes of these three who encounter Jesus. Maybe it is just as well. If they said no, we might feel a sense of superiority over those who turn down Jesus. If they said yes, we might imagine their situation really doesn't correspond to our family ties and obligations today. By leaving these encounters open-ended, Luke forces the consideration: what of us? What takes priority in our lives, even over following Jesus? Where is our ministry compromised by hands gripping the steering wheel with eyes mesmerized by the view in the rearview mirror?

The road behind may *witness* to God. But only the road ahead *leads* to God.

Direct my hands, O God, for your hands fashioned all; guide my eyes, O Christ, for you are the light of all; shape my will, O Spirit, for you are the power of all.

Encountering Jesus Today

Think about the image of looking backward with your hand on the plow or the contrasting views of windshield and rearview mirror. Then consider a situation in your life or your church that is complicated by this tension. What draws you and/or others to keep looking back? What would a "windshield larger than a rearview mirror" mean in practical terms for this situation? Prayerfully seek God's guidance in setting your eyes—and life—on the future God opens before you.

DAY FOUR

"You are not far from the kingdom of God."

How do you understand the words "not far from" spoken by Jesus to this scribe—as praise, as encouragement, as threat?

Their context in Mark points clearly in the direction of encouragement and praise. Before and after this narrative, Jesus' encounters with a variety of religious leaders are filled with conflict, entrapment, and ulterior motives. Yet here we find one of those very leaders asking a question out of admiration for Jesus. The scribe responds enthusiastically when Jesus affirms the practice of love pre-eminent in the Torah's commands. To which Jesus replies, "You are not far from the kingdom of God." That is a long way from Jesus' calling other religious officials hypocrites, whitewashed tombs, and blind guides (see Matt. 23:13-29). But "not far from" still infers a gap, a bit of daylight showing between where this scribe is and where he might be. What is to account for that gap? And does this scribe bridge it?

As to the latter question, the answer eludes us. We do not have a record from an early Christian community with this scribe on the baptismal roll. Nor do we have any proof that he remained "not far from" but never "part of" God's sovereign realm. Whether this individual bridged the gap remains unknown.

As to the question of what accounts for that gap between "not far from" and "part of" God's realm, we do not have any direct evidence for this individual. But we do have the words Jesus spoke about the primacy of love in answer to the question of what commandment is "first." And those words may suggest, indirectly, where that gap may lie for this scribe—and for us all.

Jesus begins by reciting the Shema ("Hear, O Israel: the Lord our God, the Lord is One"), the confession that faithful Jews offer at the beginning and end of each day. Jesus then combines two commandments to express what is first of all: love of God and love of neighbor as self. The scribe affirms Jesus' answer, declaring it exceeds "all burnt offerings and sacrifices," the basis of that day's Temple observances. Jesus avers that the scribe answers wisely.

Everyone seems to be in agreement—so where is the gap? Why say "not far from" rather than "you've arrived"? To me, the hint comes in the theme of this conversation: love. Love can be discussed, dissected, defined, debated, ad nauseam. But for love to be fulfilled, and thus for the commandment to be kept: love must be *done*. Paul says as much when he writes about love in 1 Corinthians 13 using *action* terms. In an intriguing connection, when Paul sums up love as the "greatest" among faith and hope, he uses the same word that appears in Mark 12:31 ("there is no other commandment *greater* than these" [emphasis added]). The greatness of love comes in its fulfillment of Torah and its expression of God's central disposition toward creation ("For God so loved the world . . ." [John 3:16]).

To me, the practice of love closes the gap between "not far from" and "part of" God's realm for this scribe and for us. I hear Jesus speaking "not far from" to the scribe, and to us, like a teacher coaxing a student into taking that next step from information to wisdom. I hear Jesus speaking "not far from" to the scribe, and to us, like a parent encouraging a child into taking that next step from freedom to responsibility. I hear Jesus speaking "not far from" to the scribe, and to us, to urge love that moves from right concept to right conduct. I hear Jesus speaking "not far from" to this scribe, and to us, as an encouragement to fulfill love rather than as a looming threat of judgment.

This last point and the text as a whole call to my mind two songs that bear the same name: "Almost Persuaded." The first I remember from Sunday school; it originated in nineteenth-century revivalism. The second comes from 1960s country-western music.

The "religious" one has words that spiral down into a mournful ending: "Sad, sad, that bitter wail—'Almost,' but lost!" The secular title starts on a despairing note, involving a bar and a married man attracted to someone other than his wife. But this second "Almost Persuaded" ends with the practice of love that keeps covenant and fidelity.

The gospel song's faith-as-fear approach may seek to scare the hell out of us. But when it comes to the love Jesus taught and commanded, the honky-tonk number has the truth hands down. "You are not far from the kingdom of God" is not a brimstone-laden threat held over our heads by a God itching to catch us red-handed. Rather, it is a grace-laden invitation calling our hearts and wills to take that next step from love's right understanding to its right practice.

Grace me, O God, to move from love's knowledge to love's practice, in Jesus Christ.

Encountering Jesus Today

Read the words "you are not far from the kingdom of God" aloud, as if Jesus addressed them to you. Where do they speak to you on your spiritual journey at this moment? That is, where do they speak the truth about you're being on the right track . . . but needing something more? Focus on what that "something more" might be, particularly in moving from words of love to enacting love. Translate that movement into terms as practical as you can. Pray for Spirit's leading in moving closer to the life and love God seeks from and for you—and through you.

DAY FIVE

The Crowd   *Matthew 7:28-29*

It could be argued that the character most frequently encountered by Jesus in the Gospels is *the crowd*. Its composition changes, to be sure. The crowd in Galilee is not made up of the same folks as the crowd in Jerusalem. Besides composition, the crowd's disposition changes as well. The crowd at one juncture desires to make Jesus king (John 6:15), while at another seeks to toss Jesus off the nearest cliff (Luke 4:29). To say that the crowd is fickle is an understatement. Yet, the Gospels' crowd has no corner on that market. Witness the disciples' flight from Gethsemane when the going got tough. The crowd, like the disciples, reflects the sometimes conflicting truths of human nature.

For those reasons and more, this chapter and book close with consideration of the "character" named *the crowd*. In terms of this chapter, the crowd portrays the open-ended nature of encounters with Jesus more than any other character. The crowd always seems to be on the fringe. It may be astonished; it may be hostile; it may even be Jesus' last viable defense against authorities set to take him down except for their fear of the crowd. But in the end, we have no clear word on where the gospeling of the crowd leads them. The Gospels do not say what became of the crowds who encountered Jesus: the one fed with loaves and fishes, the one welcoming his entry with palm branches and hosannas, the one crying out for his crucifixion. The crowd remains anonymous and undecided. Those who stake the claim to faith and those who stake others on crosses have decided yes or no to the call of Jesus. The crowd, on the other hand, keeps to the edges of the action. Others play out the gospel. The crowd waits and sees.

The crowd provides the closing word and character for this book because, as readers and listeners to the Gospel narratives, we share much in common with the crowd. We are, like the crowd, spectators to the Gospels' unfolding story. Like the crowd, we stand on the edge and watch these encounters with Jesus. At times, that gives us an advantage, particularly when the narrative makes us privy to information not available to those first eyewitnesses. Hindsight is always better than foresight. At times, though, the advantage turns to disadvantage. Because we know things ahead of time—or, at least, we *think* we do—those encounters may seem long ago and far removed from our present-day circumstances. Like the crowd in Jesus' time, detachment from the story can seduce us into thinking it is a story about the decisions of others.

But while the crowd may remain on the outside looking in at these encounters with Jesus, and in doing so may exhibit a certain indifference to the gospel, the gospel is not indifferent to the crowd. In truth, these encounters with Jesus intend to draw us—as they attempted to draw the crowd—into the narrative for the sake of decision and commitment.

I find it intriguing that in the Gospels the words for *crowd* and *multitude* occur throughout the story—except at the end. There is not a single reference to "crowd" after Good Friday. On the one hand, that is understandable. What's to gather a crowd after the center of interest has gone and got himself killed? But even after Easter's raising, none of the Gospels uses the word *crowd*. After Easter, the time for detached witnesses who sit on the fence rail of impartiality has passed. After Easter, the gospel lifts up the witness of courageous women, whose words fly in the face of conventional wisdom. After Easter, the gospel focuses on once-cowering disciples who, transformed by Spirit's gift into apostles turn the world upside down with their proclamation and with their love.

Put another way, the crowd disappears between Good Friday and Easter so that another community may emerge. Jesus calls out this new community from the anonymity of the crowd, and in that calling, christens it—christens us—with a new name. In Greek, the word for "called out" is *ekklesia*. It is the word usually translated "church": the ones called out by Jesus.

We are the people, we are the community, called out by encounter with Jesus:

- the called-out community of Jesus
  christened to replace the indifference of the crowd with the passion of followers;
- the called-out community of Jesus
  christened to transform spectators in a crowd to participants in the gospel's drama;
- the called-out community of Jesus
  christened to trade the fickleness of crowds with fidelity to love in word and deed.

We are the people, we are the community, gospeled by encounter with Jesus!

Holy and Loving God, for encounters that gospel our lives with the grace of Jesus and the power of the Spirit, I give you thanks. Amen.

ENCOUNTERING JESUS TODAY

Consider the differences between being part of a crowd and part of a community. With those distinctions in mind, consider your own spiritual journey at this moment. Where do you hang back, seeking the anonymity or indifference of the crowd, in your faith? Where do you find the gospel "calling you out" from being part of a crowd to participating in Jesus' community? Prayerfully consider what you might do this week that would reveal your calling in Christ.

Leader's Guide

INTRODUCTION

THESE SESSION OUTLINES will aid groups who use *Gospeled Lives* as a resource in the season of Lent. The study's six sessions build through Lent, covering one chapter per week. Participants are asked to read the appropriate chapter and do the accompanying "Encountering Jesus Today" exercises in the week *prior* to the group meeting. Make sure participants have the books at least one week ahead of the first session, with instructions to do the reading and exercises for Week One. You might meet as a group the week prior to the first session (after an Ash Wednesday service, if you have one) to distribute the materials, walk through the structure of the book, read and discuss the prologue, and explain about the readings and exercises to be done each week. Sessions are designed for a forty-five-minute gathering. Each session consists of six parts:

1. Preparing
2. Opening
3. Reflecting
4. Exploring
5. Enacting
6. Closing

PREPARING includes suggestions for readying the room, gathering needed materials, and your own preparations as leader. OPENING introduces the theme. REFLECTING considers the readings and "Encountering Jesus Today" exercises of the past week. Do not gloss over or rush through the REFLECTING time. Insights shared here may present unexpected perspectives not anticipated in the session guide that merit extended attention and perhaps alteration of the session. EXPLORING delves into one aspect of the weekly theme. ENACTING invites action on the part of the participants, individually and/or as a group, in response to the theme. CLOSING summarizes and reflects on the group experience, makes any assignments, and closes with a liturgical act.

Thank you for your leadership! May these stories of and reflections on encounter with Jesus deepen the Lenten journey you and others will make—and open you to the transformation of encounters with Christ today.

Materials Needed for Most Sessions

- Bibles
- Newsprint, markers
- Glue sticks
- Paper, pencils, colored pencils, markers

FOR EACH SESSION:

> Create a worship center using a table or bench, six candles, and cloth. The gatherings are intended to be not just "head" experiences but "heart" experiences. Opening and closing the sessions around a worship center will affirm that encounter with Jesus calls us into holy presence as well as holy knowledge.

WEEK ONE / CALLED

PREPARING

Preparing to Focus

This session focuses on how encounter with Jesus in the lives of these biblical characters, and in our lives, presents an experience of call that invites response.

Preparing Yourself

Read Week One of *Gospeled Lives*. Do each of the "Encountering Jesus Today" exercises. Think about experiences you have had, as an individual and as part of a faith community, that you associate with being called. In what ways did you and/or others sense that call came out of encounter with Christ? What response was evoked, and given?

Review this session guide early in the week to allow adequate preparation of its activities. In doing so, your own reflections on the chapter's daily readings and exercises will shape those plans as you proceed through the week. Pray for the participants who will be coming, expected and unexpected. Pray that God's Spirit will equip and guide you in your leadership role.

Preparing the Space and Materials

In the middle of the worship center table, place six candles of different sizes and shapes. Have a lighter available. Place objects and/or images on the worship center that suggest "call" and relate to this week's stories. For example: fishing net; photograph/poster of a socially or economically diverse group of people; a large question mark; an image of an individual carrying a heavy load; "come and see. . ." written on a large sheet of construction paper.

Opening

- Greet participants as they enter. Gather around or in front of the worship center and ask individuals to introduce themselves to the group by saying their name and, in a sentence or less, what brings them to participate in this group.

- Light one of the candles on the worship center. Ask for one or more volunteers to read aloud the three introductory paragraphs of the "Overview" for Week One (page 17). Affirm that this opening session for exploring *Gospeled Lives* focuses on how encounter with Jesus results in an experience of call that seeks response. Note that what individuals said in introducing themselves to the group in itself expresses a response to call. Sometimes we may not be aware at the moment of all that is involved in such calls, or in the responses that unfold. But being open to hear ourselves and our communities called by God is the starting point of faith and spiritual formation. This openness is also the starting point for exploring encounters with Jesus that "gospel" our lives with call.

- Offer these or similar words in prayer:

Holy God, your voice called into the void, and creation came forth. Call us now into new life. Call to us through scripture's story. Call to us through one another's insights and questions. Call to us in this time together in word and action and silence. In all these ways, and others we may not even be aware of, call us in the Christ who still comes and seeks our good and our response. Amen.

Reflecting

- Ask participants to reflect on the daily readings and exercises from Week One.

Have individuals share with the group what spoke most deeply to them in terms of affirmations, questions, or disagreements.

If you have a large group (more than twelve persons), form small groups to allow individuals more time to speak. If you do form small groups, gather everyone and let groups report briefly on their conversations.

• Discuss ways these encounters with Jesus and the theme of "Called" connect with: (1) the season of Lent; (2) the lives and faith of the participants; (3) concerns and events in your congregation, the wider community, and the world.

EXPLORING

• Have participants choose partners. Ask individuals to share with their partner an experience of call related to their faith. Talk about such aspects as: how you "heard" or experienced the call; what or who helped you decide how (whether) you would respond; how the experience shaped your understanding of call.

• Gather everyone together. Ask partners to briefly summarize their conversations and insights. Invite the group to identify common themes and experiences that emerge in these reports. Note these commonalities on newsprint. Encourage participants to add ideas they consider crucial to "call," whether from this week's readings or their own experience.

ENACTING

• Engage the group in considering ways your church could help individuals and groups in discerning and responding to such experiences of call. Begin by identifying ways your church currently provides such help. On the newsprint sheet(s) created previously, put a check mark beside comments where your church is actively engaged in supporting call's discernment or response. Put a question mark beside comments where support or help is uncertain. Circle comments where a clear need exists for the church to provide support or guidance.

- Prioritize and perhaps combine the items circled or the question marks: where is the church's most pressing need to help individuals and groups in discerning and responding to faith callings? Work together as a group to develop at least a tentative idea or proposal that would be a first step in this direction. Identify the person or group in the church to receive the proposal, and determine how to present it. Covenant together to take this proposal to the appropriate congregational leadership.

- In making this covenant, remind the participants they may lead by example. Encourage them, individually and collectively (through this Lenten study, for example), to practice discerning calls that come from faith and encounter with Christ more intentionally and to respond with greater openness to those calls.

Closing

- Gather everyone at the worship center. Note the symbols and/or images on the table that remind us of the call stories from the past week. Such Biblical stories of call point us toward the God who encounters us where we live in our day. In this time together call has also taken shape in conversations and discussions. Call has been given form in the ideas generated to pass on to the wider church that we might together be more discerning and responsive to the calls God in Christ still brings our way. Invite participants to share how this session has shaped their understanding of being called.

- Close by singing a song (or reading their stanzas in litany form) about the call that comes in encounter with Jesus and our response. Possibilities include "Two Fishermen" ("Leave All Things You Have"); "The Summons" ("Will You Come and Follow Me"); "Jesus Calls Us"; "You Walk Along Our Shoreline."

- Remind everyone to read Week Two, one reading each day, and to do the related "Encountering Jesus Today" exercises. Invite participants to bring pictures or symbols of something they consider to be "challenging." Make any other necessary announcements about the next meeting or preparation for it.

Week Two / Challenged

Preparing

Preparing to Focus

This session explores how encounter with Jesus, in the lives of these biblical characters and in our own experience, brings challenges to adopt new ways of trusting, welcoming, and serving.

Preparing Yourself

Read Week Two of *Gospeled Lives*. Do each of the "Encountering Jesus Today" exercises. Think back on experiences when faith or spiritual growth has been a challenge for you: not only in matters of belief or trust but in conduct and behavior. What created that challenge? In what ways did faith or a sense of "Christ-encounter" allow you to take on that challenge? What might have held you back from that challenge?

Review this session guide early in the week to allow adequate preparation of its activities. In doing so, your own reflections on the chapter's daily readings and exercises will shape those plans as you proceed through the week. Pray for the participants who will be coming, expected and unexpected. Pray that God's Spirit will equip and guide you in your leadership role.

Preparing the Space and Materials

In the middle of the worship center table, place six candles of different sizes and shapes. Have a lighter or matches available. Leave room on or near the worship center to display images and symbols of "challenge" that participants were asked to bring at the end of the last session. Bring your own image or symbol. You may want to send a midweek reminder about the assignment to bring symbols, and you also could have some on hand to choose from.

OPENING

- Greet participants as they enter. Have them place their symbol or image on or near the worship center.

- Light two of the candles on the worship center (one should be the candle lit for the previous session). Have participants identify the symbol or image they brought, and in a sentence or two describe how it speaks to them about the theme of challenge. Ask one or more volunteers to read the overview for Week Two on page 35. Invite reflection and discussion on how those words of challenge that arise out of encounter with Jesus relate to the symbols and images brought by the participants. Encourage individuals to keep these symbols and images in mind as you explore together the challenges to faith by encounters with Jesus: through the stories of scripture, through conversation with others, and through personal experience.

- Offer these or similar words in prayer:

  Open us, O God, to your coming among us: through word, through Spirit, through one another. Keep our faith resilient when your coming challenges us to new ways and new thoughts—and new persons. Guide us in this time together, and may it prepare us for our times apart—that we may be equipped for the challenges you bring for the sake of your coming realm. In Jesus Christ. Amen.

REFLECTING

- Ask participants to reflect on the daily readings and exercises from Week Two.

  - Have individuals share with the group what spoke most deeply to them in terms of affirmations, questions, or disagreements.

  - If you have a large group (more than twelve persons), form small groups to allow individuals more time to speak. If you do form small groups, gather everyone and let groups report briefly on their conversations.

- Discuss ways in which these stories and readings of encounter with Jesus and the theme of "Challenged" connect with: the season of Lent; the lives and faith of the participants; concerns and events in your congregation, the wider community, and the world.

EXPLORING

- Have each participant write about a current challenge in his or her life (in a journal or on paper supplied). Assure group members that they will not have to disclose this situation or the journal entry to others. Suggest that the journal entry to reflect on: (1) what makes this so challenging for you; and (2) what connections might exist between this challenge and your faith (for example: how might faith be a resource for addressing the challenge and/or how faith itself may be part of the challenge). Allow no more than ten minutes for this exercise.

- Without specifying the nature of this challenge, invite willing participants to reflect on these connections between the challenge(s) faced and the faith that comes from encounter with God.

ENACTING

- Say these or similar words: *Challenge is a natural part of life and a natural part of faith. Encounter with Jesus engages us on any number of levels: to trust more deeply, to serve more graciously, to love unconditionally. The stories this week reveal these challenges, as do our own experiences of faithful encounter with Jesus. And what holds true for individuals holds true for Christian community: encounter with Jesus summons Christian community to mature and change.*

- Invite people to brainstorm areas where the church is being challenged today. You might start with "the church" in general to get ideas flowing, but do not leave the conversation in generalities that can disarm the challenge. Move the discussion to specific areas where your faith community finds itself challenged. Narrow the conversation to one challenge. How does faith, and encounter with God, bring resources to help you deal with the challenge; and how does the challenge grow out of that faith and encounter?

- Identify two or three ways the group might take action in response to the challenge in your community's life. You may wish to form two or three small groups by allowing participants to self-select which to join, to draw up several concrete steps in concert with or as a vanguard to wider congregational response. Gather the groups to review these ideas for action and what will be done in this coming week to address this challenge. Encourage the participants to covenant together, whether as individuals working separately or in groups.

CLOSING

- Gather at the worship center. Invite the group to reflect how this session has deepened their awareness about the inevitable challenge of living faithfully for individuals and communities of faith. Elicit connections with those symbols and images of challenge brought to this session.

- Close by singing a song (or using its stanzas as a litany or responsive reading) about the challenge brought to our lives and communities by encounter with Jesus. Possibilities include "Gather Us In"; "What Does the Lord Require of You"; "They'll Know We Are Christians by Our Love."

- Remind everyone to read Week Three, one reading each day, and to do the related daily exercises. Make any other necessary announcements about the next meeting or preparation for it.

WEEK THREE / REJECTED

PREPARING

Preparing to Focus

This session explores how encounter with Jesus, in the lives of these biblical characters and in our own experience, allows for the possibility of rejection as well as acceptance.

Preparing Yourself

Read Week Three of *Gospeled Lives*. Do each of the "Encountering Jesus Today" exercises. Consider times when you have seen faith or discipleship rejected: out of expediency, out of opposition, or out of other motivations you can name. Reflect on when you have rejected a hard or difficult call of faith. What did you learn from that experience? How has it shaped your following of Jesus today?

Review this session guide early in the week to allow adequate preparation of its activities. In doing so, your own reflections on the chapter's daily readings and exercises will shape those plans as you proceed through the week. Pray for the participants who will be coming, expected and unexpected. Pray that God's Spirit will equip and guide you in your leadership role.

Preparing the Space and Materials

In the middle of the worship center table, place six candles of different sizes and shapes. Have a lighter or matches available. Place objects and/or images on the worship center suggestive of "rejection," growing out of this week's stories. For example: a scene of family discord; a large dollar sign; a scene of political deal making; a basin of water (option: also a wet washrag with red stains). If available, secure the music "King Herod's Song" from *Jesus Christ Superstar* to play when folks reflect on the symbols and images of rejection in the opening (see below). Gather art materials for use in "Exploring" (colored construction paper, marking pens of various colors, scissors, glue sticks, and other craft materials available at your church).

OPENING

- Greet participants by name as they enter. Gather around or near the worship center.

- Light three of the candles on the worship center (two should be those candles lit for the previous session). Have one or more volunteers read the overview for Week Three on page 51. Affirm that the theme of rejection is not easy to deal with; but if we could not reject the gospel or encounter with Jesus, it would mean we had no choice. God has fashioned us with free will. These stories (and personal experience) reveal that God in Christ respects that freedom to say no as well as yes.

- Offer these or similar words in prayer:

Gracious God, in Christ you invite us into faith and relationship, but you leave the door open to enter or leave. In Spirit, you offer the gift of comfort and guidance, but you do not force the gift upon us against our will. Open us now to these stories of those who said no to you. May we discern the motives that may have led to those rejections, the opportunities missed . . . and above all, your presence that allows no for the sake of a yes that truly matters. In Jesus Christ. Amen.

REFLECTING

- Ask participants to reflect on the daily readings and exercises from Week Three.

  - Have individuals share with the group what spoke most deeply to them in terms of affirmations, questions, or disagreements.

  - If you have a large group (more than twelve persons), form small groups to allow individuals more time to speak. If you do form small groups, gather everyone and let groups report briefly on their conversations.

- Discuss ways these stories and readings of encounter with Jesus and the theme of "Rejected" connect with: the season of Lent; the lives and faith experience of the participants; concerns and events in your congregation, the wider community, and the world.

EXPLORING

- If available, play a recording of "King Herod's Song" from *Jesus Christ Superstar*. Discuss how the song, along with the images and symbols of rejection on the worship center, connect with contemporary experiences of rejection related to faith.

- Invite participants to work individually or with partners, using materials provided, to create symbols or images that reflect how rejection of encounter with Jesus plays out today. Place their creations on the worship center along with those placed there at the outset. Ask individuals and partners willing to do so to offer brief comments on what they have placed there. Given the difficulty of this theme, affirm that no one needs to speak or share anything that makes them uncomfortable.

ENACTING

- Have group members reflect on the encounters explored in this chapter. On one sheet of newsprint, identify what generates these experiences of rejection. On another sheet of newsprint, brainstorm the consequences of that rejection: for the character or group involved, for Jesus, for the wider community. Discuss how these causes and consequences relate to contemporary experiences in the church and community.

- Have the group select the one cause of rejection in these encounters with Jesus that seems to them most contemporary: in terms of faith and community today, in terms of their own struggles and journey in faith. Working in groups of three or four, identify ways in which your congregation might respond to these causes. Consider also how a sincere no may be more revealing and genuine than an insincere yes when it comes to encounter with Jesus or even participation in the church.

- Gather the groups and invite summaries of their conversations and insights. Decide how and to whom to take ideas and suggestions for consideration by the wider church community. Also talk about what participants might do in response to these conversations.

CLOSING

- Gather the group in a circle at the worship center. Reflect on what this session has stirred in minds and hearts about the theme of rejection in encounter with Jesus—and in our own faith experience. Invite individuals who are willing to share with the others the most significant insight from this time.

  Sing "Would I Have Answered When You Called."

- Close with a sentence prayer, in which each individual offers a simple prayer related to this session's experience. Join hands. Explain you will begin the prayer yourself, then squeeze the hand of the person to your right. That person then offers a sentence prayer and squeezes the hand of the next person to the right. If someone does not feel comfortable praying aloud, a squeeze of the hand to the right signifies a pass. Close the prayer when the circle is completed.

- Remind everyone to read Week Four, one reading each day, and to do the related daily exercises. Make announcements about the next meeting (time, place, any special assignment or preparation).

WEEK FOUR / TRANSFORMED

PREPARING

Preparing to Focus

This session explores how encounter with Jesus, in the lives of these biblical characters and in our own experience, promises transformation intended to change us for the good.

Preparing Yourself

Read Week Four of *Gospeled Lives*. Do each of the "Encountering Jesus Today" exercises.

Look back on experiences you would see as transformative in the lives of others and in your own experience. What generated such change, and the risk that often accompanies it? Where and how has such transformation been part of your spiritual journey? How do see this transformation resulting from your encounter with the Holy?

Review this session guide early in the week to allow adequate preparation of its activities. In doing so, your own reflections on the chapter's daily readings and exercises will shape those plans as you proceed through the week. Pray for the participants who will be coming, expected and unexpected. Pray that God's Spirit will equip and guide you in your leadership role.

Preparing the Space and Materials

In the middle of the worship center table, place six candles of different sizes and shapes. Have a lighter or matches available. Gather symbols or images of "transformation" to place on the worship center and/or around your meeting space. Rather than symbols related to this chapter's stories of encounter, seek ones that reflect transformation in your own setting. They might be images or symbols related to the history of or recent events in your church and community. The symbols might come from your natural environment (a caterpillar or cocoon). Be creative. Imagine what the participants might see as a sign of transformation in your midst.

OPENING

- Greet participants by name as they enter. Invite them to browse the symbols and images you have set out and silently reflect on what they individually and collectively bring to mind and heart. When all have gathered, ask participants to comment briefly on what they see in these images and symbols.

- Light four of the candles on the worship center (three should be candles lit for the previous session). Have one or more volunteers read the overview for Week Four on page 67. Make connections, if not already expressed in the opening conversation, between the symbols and images and the theme of transformation. Underscore the overview's point about transformation as change. Affirm that change does not always come easily. We may seek the gospel's transformation of some parts of our lives but not others. Encourage participants to be open in this session both to the possibilities brought by transformation as well as its more difficult aspects in our lives and in community.

- Offer these or similar words for prayer:

God of healing and turning: form and transform us according to your good purposes, for us and for all. In Jesus Christ. Amen.

REFLECTING

- Ask participants to reflect on the daily readings and exercises from Week Four.

- Have individuals share with the group what spoke most deeply to them in terms of affirmations, questions, or disagreements.

- If you have a large group (more than twelve persons), form small groups to allow individuals more time to speak. If you do form small groups, gather everyone and let groups report briefly on their conversations.

• Discuss ways in which these stories and readings of encounter with Jesus and the theme of "Transformed" connect with the season of Lent; the lives and faith experience of the participants; concerns and events in your congregation, the wider community, and the world.

EXPLORING

• Invite participants to recall silently an experience in their faith they consider transformative. Read the following questions, pausing between them to allow time for reflection. *What made that experience transformative for you? . . . What was changed in your life as well as your faith? . . . What was the ease or difficulty of the transformation at that time? How does this experience continue to shape you?* . . . Allow several minutes for silent meditation.

• Form pairs. Invite partners to share what each feels comfortable revealing from these thoughts and remembrances. Say that you will give two minutes for each, and announce starting and stopping times, so that one person does not take up the whole period. Encourage partners to listen carefully to each other.

• Gather the group. Invite individuals and/or partners to note common themes or insights about the experience of transformation from these times of sharing.

ENACTING

- Read aloud the "Encountering Jesus Today" activity that follows the story of the widow of Nain (fourth reading in chapter). Review the theme and meaning of compassion as explored in that reading and encouraged in that activity.

- Invite the group to discuss in what ways your congregation is a community of compassion. Insist that the discussion on compassion not relate only to what the church thinks about compassion but also what it does in concrete and specific ways. Identify one current situation in which the church could practice compassion more effectively. What form could compassion take in that setting?

- Discuss how your group could work to raise this issue with appropriate leadership in the congregation. Beyond that, decide how you, individually and as a group, will spearhead that compassionate response. What can and will you do in the next week to demonstrate compassion that brings transformation?

CLOSING

- Gather at the worship center. Recall the symbols of transformation displayed there and around the room, and the way in which they suggest the encounters considered this week. Invite participants to reflect aloud on what they have learned, experienced, and/or remembered of transformation through this session that they will carry with them through this week. Affirm that transformation comes as both an act of God's grace and a commitment of human will. Our openness to God and one another forms the path between God's grace and our action.

- Close by singing a song or hymn whose theme is transformation. Possibilities include "Hymn of Promise" ("In the bulb there is a flower"); "Blest Are They"; "My Life Flows On" ("How Can I Keep from Singing").

- Remind everyone to read Week Five, one reading each day, and to do the related daily exercises. Make announcements about the next meeting (time, place, any special assignment or preparation).

WEEK FIVE / EMPOWERED

PREPARING

Preparing to Focus

This session explores how encounter with Jesus intends to empower us for the practice of faith and ministry in our lives and in service to others.

Preparing Yourself

Read Week Five of *Gospeled Lives*. Do each of the "Encountering Jesus Today" exercises.

Recall an experience in your spiritual journey that you found empowering. What made it so, and through whom did that empowerment come? What action or direction did it make possible for you Give thanks to God for the gift of such experiences!

Review this session guide early in the week to allow adequate preparation of its activities. In doing so, your own reflections on the chapter's daily readings and exercises will shape those plans as you proceed through the week. Pray for the participants who will be coming, expected and unexpected. Pray that God's Spirit will equip and empower you in your leadership role.

Preparing the Space and Materials

In the middle of the worship center table, place six candles of different sizes and shapes. Have a lighter or matches available. Have craft and art materials available to create symbols of power (see "Opening" below). Materials could include, but not be limited to pipe cleaners of various colors, modeling clay, watercolors, plain paper, and construction paper.

OPENING

- Greet participants by name as they enter. Invite them to look around the room and out the windows (if you have some). Ask: *Where do you see sources of power around you in this place? What do these sources of power make possible for you or others?* Have participants create a symbol of one of those sources of power using the art and craft materials. As each person completes this work, place the symbol on the worship space. When all are done, ask individuals to identify their symbol and what its power makes possible.

  Light five of the candles on the worship center (four should be candles lit for the previous session). Have one or more volunteers read the overview for Week Five on page 83. Affirm today's theme of empowerment, represented by the symbols on the worship center and reflected in the readings related to this week's chapter. Encourage participants as you proceed through the conversations and activities in this session to be mindful of the ways even this gathering brings power to their lives for the sake of both personal growth and ministry for others.

- Offer these or similar words for prayer:

Holy God, we see your hand in creation—where you set your power toward the fashioning of life and community. In Christ you revealed your love in acts of power that healed and restored and freed. In Spirit you dwell among us to empower your people to do the service to which you call us. In Jesus Christ. Amen.

REFLECTING

- Ask participants to reflect on the daily readings and exercises from Week Five.

    - Have individuals share with the group what spoke most deeply to them in terms of affirmations, questions, or disagreements.

    - If you have a large group (more than twelve persons), form small groups to allow individuals more time to speak. If you do form small groups, gather everyone and let groups report briefly on their conversations.

- Discuss how these stories of encounter with Jesus and the theme of "Empowered" connect with the season of Lent; the lives and faith experience of the participants; concerns and events in your congregation, the wider community, and the world.

EXPLORING

- Give each participant a blank sheet of paper. Ask everyone to draw a line down the sheet lengthwise. Label the one side: "encounter with Jesus empowers me to." Label the other side: "encounter with Jesus empowers me not to." Invite people to make lists for each column based on their personal experience. Allow no more than three minutes. At the end of that time, ask individuals to look over the lists they have created. Invite reflection on how the items on one list are related to those on the other list, and why.

- Form groups of three or four. Discuss what individuals discerned about relationships between the two lists. Affirm that people need not share specifics of what they wrote if they do not feel comfortable doing so.

- Gather the group. Invite comments and insights about how we experience empowerment in our spiritual journeys as revealed in the lists and group discussions.

ENACTING

- Review the way in which this chapter's readings approach the theme of empowerment from various angles: as the gift that enables our practice of vocation (Peter's Mother-in-Law); through the ability to take on what we might not have chosen on our own (Gerasene Demoniac); by our support of those whose presence or even ministry may otherwise go undervalued (Mary Magdalene and "Many Others"); in the gift of acceptance that leads to change in the welcomed one (Zacchaeus); by the companions with whom we feel comfortable sharing our faith journey in deep ways (Emmaus Road Disciples).

- Invite participants to choose one of those five focuses on empowerment for further reflection and action. Have them work together with others who made the same choice. (If one or more focuses have no one working on them, that is fine! Let folks work where they feel drawn.) Instruct each group to use the "Encountering Jesus Today" exercise that matches the chosen focus/character. Rather than doing the exercise individually, as they did during the week, work on that activity as a group.

- Gather the groups. Invite them to summarize insights from the small-group work and briefly identify one or more actions they will individually and collectively do in response.

CLOSING

- Gather at the worship center. Invite participants to call out words or phrases concerning the theme of empowerment brought out in this session. Affirm that empowerment underscores the truth that God does not leave us alone or unaided to live out the faith and exercise the ministries to which we have been called. We have the gift of God's Spirit. We have the presence and encouragement of Christian community. We have the peculiar gifts with which God has graced each one of us. And God gathers together for the sake of our doing the work of Christ.

- Close by singing a song with the theme of empowerment. Possibilities include "Spirit, Spirit of Gentleness," "Let Us Talents and Tongues Employ," "God Whose Giving Knows No Ending."

- Remind everyone to read Week Six, one reading each day, and to do the related daily exercises. Make announcements about the next meeting (time, place, any special assignment or preparation).

WEEK SIX / OPEN-ENDED

PREPARING

Preparing to Focus

This session explores how encounter with Jesus always has been and always will be an open-ended opportunity that invites but does not predetermine our decision to follow.

Preparing Yourself

Read Week Six of *Gospeled Lives*. Do each of the "Encountering Jesus Today" exercises. Call to mind an important juncture where you faced a "fork in the road" in your faith journey. Which path did you choose, and which did you not? Why? In what ways did that decision open more doors than it closed (or close more than it opened) and shape ensuing decisions you have made?

Review this session guide early in the week to allow adequate preparation of its activities. In doing so, be open to how your own reflections on the chapter's daily readings and exercises might shape those plans for the session. Pray for the participants who will be coming, especially for any who may be facing significant choices in their lives and faith. Pray for openness, your own and that of the participants, to the presence and leading of God's Spirit in your gathering for the concluding session of this study.

Preparing the Space and Materials

In the middle of the worship center table, place six candles of different sizes and shapes. Have a lighter or matches available. Bring an image (painting, photograph, or other artwork) that conveys to you a sense of open-endedness and journey: for example, a path that divides or a road that continues into the distance so that its end is hidden. Place it on the worship center.

Opening

- Greet participants by name as they enter. When all are present, gather around or in front of the worship center. View the image you placed there. Ask participants to consider silently these or similar questions: *What does this image portray? In what ways does it spark your curiosity, wonder, or fear? Where do you think this image seeks to "lead" you?*

- Invite participants to call out words or phrases that came to mind as they viewed the image and considered those questions. As they do so, light all six candles. Have one or more volunteers read the overview for Week Six on page 99. Note connections between that reading and its theme "open-ended," the image on the worship center, and the responses participants offered to it. In this final session encourage participants to be open to ways in which the conversations and activities may go with them in their future choices of faith and discipleship.

- Offer these or similar words for prayer:

God of the journey, you meet us again: in Spirit's presence, in one another's company, in this time and place of gathering. Move among us. Open our words and ears, open our minds and spirits, to what you would bring to and through us. When we encounter you outside these familiar environs, may we hear and respond with faith, with love, and choose to follow you. In Jesus Christ. Amen.

Reflecting

- Ask participants to reflect on the daily readings and exercises from Week Six.

- Have individuals share with the group what spoke most deeply to them in terms of affirmations, questions, or disagreements.

- If you have a large group (more than twelve persons), form small groups to allow individuals more time to speak. If you do form small groups, gather everyone and let groups report briefly on their conversations.

• Discuss ways in which these stories and readings of encounter with Jesus and the theme of "Open-Ended" connect with the season of Lent; the present lives and choices and faith experience of the participants; and contemporary concerns and events in your congregation, the wider community, and the world.

EXPLORING

Give each individual a slip of paper with the following quotation from the chapter's overview: *Like baptism, encounter with Jesus always has been and always will be a door opening and choices beginning.* Invite individuals to spend a few minutes reflecting silently on how those words hold true for their spiritual journey. How has their spiritual journey or times of encounter with Jesus been more of a beginning than an ending, choices just starting rather than concluding?

• Form groups of three or four to discuss this quotation in light of their personal reflections. Move the conversation to consideration of what those words might mean for the way your congregation engages in sacraments, evangelism, education, and/or spiritual growth. Gather the whole group together and share highlights of the small group conversations.

Enacting

- Based on the previous discussion and sharing, focus on what it means for your church to be a place that nurtures, encourages, and offers encounter with Jesus that "always has been and always will be a door opening and choices beginning." Let participants identify one or two areas in your church's life for cultivating open-ended encounter.

- Working as a whole group—or in two groups if the group is large or if two areas were identified—develop ideas for incorporating opportunities for such encounter in the church's program and mission. For example, using the analogy of windshields and rearview mirrors, how might your church's "windshield" be enlarged in the ways you invite people to discipleship or the ways you offer options to participate (varied versus one-size-fits-all).

- Make notes of these ideas and—just as important—how they will be presented to the community and its leaders.

Closing

- Gather at the worship center. Invite participants to affirm not only what they may have gained from this session but thoughts on all the gatherings as a whole. Affirm that participants in the group, and not just the characters in the stories, have served as examples of "gospeled lives" on this journey. Christ's presence, experienced in these stories and in this community we have shared, will continue to accompany us on the way. Thank everyone for their participation in this group and invite them to further opportunities for spiritual growth and formation your congregation may be offering now or in the future.

- Sing a song that celebrates the way God opens before us in Christ. Possibilities include "I Was There to Hear Your Borning

Cry"; "Sent Forth By God's Blessing"; "My Faith It Is an Oaken Staff."

- Close by paraphrasing the closing lines from Week Six as benediction and commission:

We are the people, we are the community, gospeled by encounter with Jesus!

We are the people, we are the community, transformed by that encounter.

Go with God's grace, live by Christ's love, rely on Spirit's power and presence.

About the Author

John Indermark is a writer and retired United Church of Christ minister. He is the author of a number of books published by Upper Room Books and Abingdon Press and has also written for a variety of curriculum resources. John and his wife, Judy, split their time between the Sonoran desert region of Tucson and the Willapa Hills rainforest in southwest Washington.

Other Upper Room books by John Indermark

Genesis of Grace

Neglected Voices

Parables and Passion

Setting the Christmas Stage

Traveling the Prayer Paths of Jesus

Turn Toward Promise

The Way of Grace

Inquire at your local bookstore

Order online: www.upperroom.org/books

Or call: 1-800-972-0433